HOW TO PLAY

Hello, Detective. Welcome to Midsomer.

The aim of the adventure you're about to undertake is simple: survive. Can you make it through a weekend in Midsomer, all while trying to get to the bottom of a murder case?

Depending on which path you take through the story, you'll uncover different clues and meet with different endings. You might solve parts of the case – possibly all of it. There are all sorts of secrets waiting for you, and lots of different outcomes.

All you need to remember is this: at the end of each passage of text, you'll be directed to the numbered section you need to read next. Most passages end in a choice: just follow the instructions and flick to the relevant section number (use the numbers at the top of the page to guide you) to continue your investigation. That's the easy bit. The trickier bit might just be staying alive.

Once you reach the end of your adventure, go to 'Your Performance Review' on **p.293** to see how well you did and get hints on what you missed, ready for your next crack at the case.

Stay safe out there – and we hope you make it through the idyllic villages of Midsomer in one piece...

COULD YOU SURVIVE MIDSOMER?

SIMON BREW

POLICE
POLICE

1

Glancing up at the skies, Veronica Woollaston breathes an audible sigh of relief.

For much of the week, the local newspaper has been forecasting heavy rain, which threatens to undo the intense months of planning and work she's put in. But the grin of the sun through the breaking clouds suggests for the first time that week that it might all be okay – just.

She allows herself a smile as she pours herself a cup of tea and takes a homemade shortbread from the tin. In twenty-four hours, Midsomer's first ever regional Villages In Bloom competition will be well under way.

She cautiously sips her tea before studiously positioning it in the centre of a pristine doily. The soft blue floral wallpaper is the only real element of fuss in a living room where everything is very much in its place.

Veronica sits down in her favourite armchair and picks up the phone. She dials her best friend, Monica Davies, and prepares to relay the good news. Between the two of them, they came up with the idea for the flower competition what feels like eighteen very long months ago. Maybe even longer than that. Since yesterday, they've been all but certain they were going to have to cancel it due to bad weather.

Oh, how well Veronica recalls the pivotal village committee meeting when they first proposed the idea. Set up at the turn of the last century, when times were tough, the committee prides itself on the support it offers local villagers such as her. She'll never forget the kindness of its members on that indelible day eighteen years ago. The tap at the door, the wave of grief that immediately engulfed her when she saw the two officers from Midsomer CID with their respectful bowed heads.

The officers' words had still shocked her, of course, when they told her how Frank had been taken from her. At least, she told her friends afterwards, he'd died doing what he loved; he was devoted to his lawnmowers. The committee had closed in around her with support, a kindness she's never forgotten.

Her bittersweet reminiscences are interrupted when Monica answers the phone. Veronica has to chuckle when Monica excitedly blurts out the weather news before even saying hello to her friend, but that's the way their decades-old friendship has always been. Monica always loves a good natter, assuming she's remembered to put her teeth in, of course.

Yet they both know this is important. After all, for Monica too, the committee has been there when she needed support in dark times. The pair may have rolled their eyes at the endless cheese-and-wine evenings, coffee mornings and infamous croquet afternoons, but they are both quietly thankful for it all. It's why they'd both instinctively known at that fateful meeting, when the dreadful state of the committee's finances were laid bare, that they had to act.

And act they had. It had been exhausting, and tempers had sometimes got frayed, but now, in the six finalist villages across Midsomer county, final preparations are being made for the biggest competition the region has seen in years. Flowers are being watered, bushes are being trimmed, rogue blooms are being plucked.

Many people are planning their visit from further afield, too, which should drum up even more funds. A picturesque, peaceful and relaxing day beckons for all, the first of what will hopefully become an annual tradition for those already starting to pack their picnics.

It should be a wonderful day, Monica and Veronica agree. The committee's financial problems will be over: not just now, but well into the future. Veronica hopes so, anyway. Because then nobody will ever have to know...

Veronica replaces the receiver and nibbles her shortbread. A little too much sugar, she thinks, and makes a mental note to adjust her recipe. But just as she lets herself relax a little, there's a knock at the door, something that never fails to bring back memories.

The story is now in your hands. Turn the page and the adventure begins: what happens next will be determined by the choices you make. There's a case to be solved. But will you solve it? Or will you become a Midsomer statistic yourself? Going forward, simply jump to the numbered section that matches your decision. For now, you can get started by going to number 77.

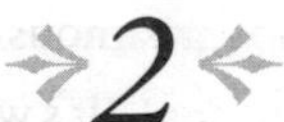

2

You start walking in the direction of Monica, who suddenly looks alarmed. She quickly composes herself and heads through a door at the back of the room marked by a bright-green exit sign. You figure she's trying to leave unnoticed, so you wait a few minutes, then go out the front door and make your way around the building as discreetly as you can. Hopefully you can talk to her without being noticed.

You spot her from across the car park. This first afternoon has whistled by, you think, noting the darkness already threatening to close in. You follow Monica down a small track around the back of the building.

'This is all a bit cloak and dagger, isn't it?' you remark as you finally make it within earshot of her.

'You can't be too careful, Detective,' she says, sounding a good deal less together than she was in the village hall. 'Villages like this one have eyes all over.'

That much you can agree on. 'Why so clandestine?' you query. 'Because of this,' she says, as she reaches into her bag. She pulls out a bland-looking cream envelope. No writing on the front, you notice, but the envelope has been opened. You pull out a small piece of paper from inside. It's empty, save for some chilling words typed across the centre of it: 'Do make sure the competition goes ahead.'

Your head is awash with questions. 'They know I'm the deputy chair of the organizing committee,' Monica reasons, pre-empting what you wanted to ask. 'They must have figured someone would try and cancel the competition, and figured I'd have some sway.'

'And do you?'

'Well, clearly not,' she says, gesturing at you. 'But that's not what people perceive.'

Her eyes keep darting behind you, aware of the risk of being seen. She's quite emotional. 'That's not all,' she whispers. A pregnant pause. 'I think Peter Maddock knew he was in some kind of danger.'

'Why do you say that?'

'Just something he said. One of my duties was to ring around the entrants for each village. He was representing Little Norton, and I spoke to him at the start of the week.'

'And what did he say to you?'

She pauses, a tear in her eye. 'Someone really doesn't want me to win this,' she whispers.

Surely that's just a bit of rivalry, though, you suggest. Winning a flower competition is hardly likely to incite someone to attack him?

'No,' agrees Monica Davies. 'But the £100,000 prize for the winning village might.'

£100,000, you think! For a village flower competition!

'Please,' she continues. 'Please reconsider. I'm already scared if it goes ahead. I dread to think what'll happen if it doesn't.'

Now what? Do you let the competition go ahead after all, knowing what you know now? If so, you're overdue a bit of rest, and you're going to be needing plenty of energy tomorrow. Call it a day for now, and go to **67**.

This note needs to be dealt with properly. Take it off Monica Davies over at **83**.

Head back to the village hall. Make sure you're seen, and check if there's anyone there worth talking to. Perhaps they know something? For that you need to go to **51**.

3

You find Veronica's name on the list and quickly click on it. It was always going to be a long shot, this. When you were in her house earlier you saw precious little sign of a computer. If memory serves, she didn't even seem to have a mobile phone. She probably still does her sums on an abacus.

Still, her name's on the list. She must have done a computer chat at some point. You admit to a little surprise when there's a ring at least. She doesn't answer it, but you've still learned something here. Veronica has some kind of electronic gadget you didn't know about, and Peter Maddock had used it to contact her.

It doesn't solve the immediate problem, of course. You're stuck upstairs in Maddock's house, and someone's making their way up the stairs. Scrub that: they're at the top of the stairs now and looking straight at you, their face shaded by a hood.

Now what?

Run for it! Get out as quickly as you can. Do that over at **18**.

You need to face this out. Go to **140**.

Your patience is starting to ebb, frustrated as much by what Mr Thomas isn't saying to you as by what he is.

'I'm going to need that name,' you demand, using your sternest voice.

He laughs. 'I don't have to give you anything.'

'I'm a police detective.'

'Yes. From what I can tell, one who was contemplating breaking into that house without any warrant or justification. Although of course you won't be doing that now, will you?'

'I need that name.'

'Am I under arrest? Have I committed a crime?'

'No.'

'Then I don't have to do anything.' He gestures at the car coming up the road. 'I presume this is your colleague?'

He's right – it's DS Lambie. But now what should you do? If you and Lambie carry on here and try and get into the property, you're going to be filmed, and you don't have a warrant.

Want to try anyway? Go to **64**.
Or do you tell Lambie to turn around and give this one up? It's one lead you've got no legal way of quickly following up.
Head to **191**.

You check in with the Chief Inspector and tell him you're just popping to the station. He gives you permission to go.

You put your foot down, and as soon as you arrive you head to your still-pretty-much-unused desk. A few taps on the computer's keyboard and it bursts into reluctant life. 'Anything you need a hand with?' says an officer you've not yet met, breezing through the office. 'Just trying to find out a bit more about Veronica Woollaston,' you say.

'If memory serves, most of the notes are bundled in with her husband. Horrible affair, that. Poor woman. You looking for anything in particular?'

'Just trying to get some background. The problem of being the new person. Everybody knows everything but me!'

'Well, just give me a shout if you need anything. I'm PC Carter.

Call me Isabel, though. I'll be at the front desk.'

You load up a stark-looking database and take her advice by calling up the file on Frank Woollaston. It's got all the details you'd instantly expect: his date of death, a sparse but to-the-point statement from Veronica, and a copy of his death certificate.

Crikey. You didn't even know lawnmowers could do that.

No pictures, though. Unusual, you think, but then it seemed pretty clear it was an accident and, perhaps understandably, who'd want to take a picture of what's described here?

Still, this isn't telling you much. The case was assigned to a Detective Ambrose, and you find Isabel Carter to see where you can find him.

'Her.'

'Her?'

'Yeah. Shirley Ambrose. Before my time, though, I'm afraid. She retired about ten years ago, I think. Still lives in the area, though. She's only five minutes up the road.'

'Won't she be at the Villages In Bloom final?'

'Might be. Don't see her about very much. I've never met her. Heard about her, though.'

Track down Shirley Ambrose at **116.**
Or for the finale of the competition, the village hall is over at **199.**

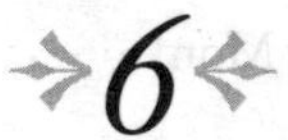

6

You dial the number you've been given for Polly Monk. She answers the phone quickly. It's a fractured line, and she's on the move. When you tell her you'd like a quick word, she's efficient and helpful, but you wouldn't go as far as to say friendly. Nonetheless, she invites you to meet her in Church Fields. She's just heading back home now.

Church Fields is a beautiful village, and as your car slips along the thin road to its main square, you feel that this place must have a strong chance of winning. As you pull up to the address Polly gave you, one small road off the square, she's standing at her front door, expecting you.

'This way,' she calls. 'People do tend to get a bit lost. Well done on finding us.'

A hot cup of coffee is waiting for you.

'I'm very sorry, Detective. I've got to leave in about 20 minutes if that's all right. The judges are coming to us first today.'

'Of course,' you say, not wanting to give her any reason not to cooperate. That said, you needn't have worried on that front. Polly is talkative and to the point.

After a few quick pleasantries, you congratulate her on the village display. 'I appreciate that,' she sighs. 'Not that we have any bloody chance of winning.'

'I don't know,' you argue. 'The village is as beautiful as any I've seen.'

She softens. 'I do appreciate that, truly. But it does feel as if this whole competition has been a done deal for a while now.'

'A done deal?'

'Well, yes. When it was first announced, I figured it was a stitch-up for the Old Norton lot.'

'Why?'

It's very clear that Polly Monk doesn't have much of a filter, and she gets to the point.

'Well, the committee is run by the iron fist of Veronica Woollaston, isn't it? And that's her village. Find me one person in Midsomer who was surprised when Old Norton ended up on the list of finalists,' she spits.

'She's not on the judging panel, though, is she?'

'She doesn't need to be. You've got her from Old Norton, and her deputy...'

'Monica Davies?'

'Yes. She's from Little Norton and they ended up on the shortlist too. The whole thing stinks. Just because they've had to absent themselves as judges doesn't mean that they weren't going to be on the list. You don't want to get on the wrong side of those two.'

'But you ended up on the list?'

'Fat lot of good it's going to do us. You only had to go to the Midsomer farmer's market last weekend to know that.'

'Something happen?'

'Peter Maddock loudly mouthing off that he was going to win. He seemed particularly confident.'

'He wasn't going to win, though, was he?'

'Even with everything that goes on behind the cardigans around here, I'd be surprised,' she smiles, trying to make light of it.

It doesn't wash with you.

'Any idea who would have killed Peter Maddock?' you say, getting up to leave.

'No,' she says, rising from her seat. 'But I can't say I'm going to miss him.'

You shake her hand and thank her for her time. 'I trust you'll be around all day if I need to ask a few more questions?'

She nods, chuckling. 'You'll know where to find me, Detective.'

You head back to the car to try and digest it all. Before you have chance, your phone bursts into life with an urgent message.
You can find it at **158**.

'I agree with you,' you say.

'About what?'

'The money. That's a lot of money for a competition like this. I've been thinking that all day. Why is the prize so big?'

'Well, I can only guess it's because somebody somewhere needs that kind of cash. Isn't that usually the reason? Lots of us would have done this for free, or for a nice bottle of wine or roll of cheese. But the committee insisted. Said it'd bring in more visitors to the area.'

'I can see their point, but even so...'

'If you ask me, the majority of problems around this area are rooted in that committee somewhere. But that's just an old lady speculating. You shouldn't pay any attention to me. I'm just going to let them get on with it.'

Right, it must be time to talk to the committee. Send a message ahead that you want to see them, and drive over to the village hall. Head to **50**.

You head up the narrow staircase, making a mental note to cross brown patterned wallpaper off your list of home décor ideas. There are only a few small rooms up here. A bathroom, what looks like a tiny office, and a bedroom. It's in the office that you see the big computer screen perched on a stand that's seen better days.

On the floor you find the main computer unit. Its lights are flashing, so you figure it must still be on. Correct. You tap on the keyboard and everything groans into life. You know how it feels.

You soon realize that Peter Maddock was quite a connected man. Icons for a chat program, various social media services and several email accounts are dotted around the screen. But it's the chat light that's blinking. You click on it, and the screen fills with a list of conversations. Most of them are fairly by the by, you conclude as you browse through them. Perfunctory chats with people to do with the competition. No real sign of family or friends.

You're drawn to one name in the list, though. Well, less a name, more one letter: X. When you click on the conversations Peter had been having with X, you can see that they're all one way. Peter never replied.

'You have to stop.'

'This has gone too far now.'

'This is your last warning. Stop.'

You grab your phone to take a photograph of the messages on his screen. As you do so, you gasp as the computer bursts into fresh life. An incoming video call. What on earth are you supposed to do now?

There's no way you can answer it. You need to get out of here, and head to the results announcement at Norton. Go to **63.**
This could be a huge clue. You've got to answer. You grab the headset from the side of the desk and click to accept the call. Go to **42.**

Your best lead is right in front of you, you figure, as they edge backwards, picking up pace. Your brain racing, you decide that you can't let them escape, and quickly begin pursuit.

But they expected it. Furthermore, the problem here is that they know the lie of the land a lot better than you. The darkness doesn't help as they dart off through the trees at the back of the hotel. You valiantly try and catch them, then realize, as you gaze at the expansive wood in front of you, that it's no good. They've gone. You stop, your eyes adjusting as best they can to the lack of light. Straining to see into the darkness, you don't immediately register the noise behind you. You certainly register the thump on the back of your head, though, which leaves you temporarily stunned. Whoever it was completes their escape in the meantime.

Resigned, with the back of your head throbbing, you realize you have little option but to call this in. Your vision is still a little blurry. You make your way back to the safety of the hotel and call the station. Not much point in them sending support now, but the motions are duly gone through.

Your colleagues aren't impressed with you. You'd best hope tomorrow goes better. It starts on **69**.

10

You look around the village hall and feel the stares of various faces in your direction. Here you are, the new Midsomer police detective, on your first day. How can you possibly try and call off a competition that clearly means a lot to everyone here? That's had so much work go into it?

At least, that's the impression you want to give people on the surface. Let them underestimate you, right? To yourself, you figure that if the competition goes ahead, you've got far more chance of solving Peter Maddock's murder.

'You're right,' you sigh, trying to convey the right mix of exasperation and inexperience in your tone. 'The competition has to go ahead.'

Let them think they've had their way.

'Of course it does,' says Veronica triumphantly, not missing a beat. She has many skills, of that you're sure. One of them, however, isn't being able to hide an innate smugness. Another small victory for her, that's how you're sure she'll see it. Still, everyone else looks relieved, too.

'I do still have to ask,' you reiterate while you have their attention, 'that if anyone knows anything about Peter Maddock and his death, no matter how minor it may appear, that you tell us. The competition is going ahead, but there's still a murderer out there.'

You detect an eye roll or two. And you're not standing for it.

'I may be new,' you snap. 'But it's my job to keep you all safe. With respect, I don't know any of you, and the murderer could even be in this very room.'

A dark hush descends. It's unlikely that your Christmas card list has been extended by your last statement.

'I will be seeing you tomorrow for the competition,' you say as you turn for the door. 'And I will be watching very closely.'

There's nothing more to say. You head back to your car and drive back to your hotel. You have a feeling it's going to be a very long day tomorrow.

Go and get some rest over on **67**, *ready for the following day.*

→11←

Now that you've got the information you need, you have to act on it quickly. You excuse yourself and call the Chief Inspector directly. It's not as if he hasn't left you a message or two as his patience starts to grow thin.

Neither of you goes for pleasantries.

'Detective, why have you been ignoring my calls?'

'Chief Inspector, I know who the murderer is.'

It'd be fair to say that very much gets his attention. You quickly relay the details and he absorbs the information with equal haste.

'This is really good work, Detective. There's one small problem to solve. Where on earth are we going to find Frank Woollaston?'

'There's a strong chance he'll have fled the area by now.'

'I figure that too. I'll send a team over to the house you and DS Lambie found in Bunbury – and we'll need to talk about proper procedure at some point, Detective. I'll come and meet you as soon as I can. If he's tying up his loose ends, then I'd imagine he might go back to Mrs Woollaston or Mr Maddock's house. But it'd be risky going back to the crime scene of either.'

He's got a point. There's so much police activity around both houses now that he's only going to go to either location if he has to.

A pause. 'Detective, I'm heading to the hospital and I'll meet you there. Let me brief everyone here and I'll be on my way. Keep yourself in plain view and safe. I hate to say it, but the only person with all the evidence at the moment to bring him down is you.'

You realize he's right, and that you're in danger. You ask him to send you the best possible picture of Frank Woollaston so you know exactly who to be on the lookout for. He does so, and you look at it, committing it quickly to memory.

But where do you go in the hospital? You're probably safer with Veronica in her hospital room. Go to **17**.
Or perhaps you're better off in plain sight. Quickly check in on Veronica, then go and sit in the busy hospital café downstairs. You'll find that at **107**.

12

You look around and conclude that the small shed in the corner of the garden is your best place to hide. If anyone appears, you should be able to spot them. Satisfied you're in a good vantage point, you get your phone out and quietly check how things are going at the hospital. Veronica Woollaston is stable, but being kept in for a day or two.

It's eerily quiet, save for the odd noise of a car trundling past. Your eyes grow heavy, resisting the coffee you've been ingesting into your system. Finally, just as you're beginning to doze, there's a noise.

Your body reawakens instantly. You peer out of the tiny window and notice a shadowy figure by the car on the road to the side. You can't spot any other vehicle. Whoever it was must be local, or must have been hiding out somewhere themselves. You creep out of the shed and see that they've opened the boot of the car. Did you miss something? As you're trying to see what could have been hidden away, you note that if anything, it looks like they're putting something in rather than taking something out. But what?

What do you do now? Confront the shadowy figure?
Do that at **97**.
Or wait for them to leave and see what they've put in the car?
That's at **201**.

13

Two murders. One woman in hospital. Precious few leads, and you can't help but feel that time is slipping away. You'll have to hope that this drive over to what feels like the middle of nowhere is worth the effort.

You're certainly some way away from the prestigious villages of Midsomer as your car passes a sign for Bunbury. It's an area that feels little run down – not one that was ever going to trouble the Villages In Bloom competition.

The address you have leads you along a bumpy road and into a nondescript cul-de-sac. A care home sits on the left as you drive in, and you swing your car around to the right where the houses sit. Number 17, the house at the end, is the one you want. Registered to a Phillip Smith.

The garden is heavily overgrown, and when you peer in through the window there's no sign of anybody inside. The curtains aren't drawn, and you can see that the living room barely has a piece of furniture in it. Why have you been sent to what looks like an abandoned house?

'No point looking in there,' says a sizeable man from across the street. You walk over and show him your ID. He suddenly looks a little shifty, but carries on talking. 'They've not been there for weeks.'

'Who's not been there?'

'Some posh woman and her son it is.'

'Son?'

'Yeah. They used to come and go, but never seemed to stay there. It's like they used the house just to meet up for a bit or something.'

Your mind is racing. 'Would you recognize the mother if I showed you a picture?'

'Suppose. Tried saying hello to them a couple of times, but they always looked like they were in a hurry.'

Quickly, you message DS Lambie, and ask him to send a bunch of pictures over. No time to explain. Just send those pictures from the entry forms or something. He's not selective, and two minutes later a few pictures of all the people involved with the Villages In Bloom competition arrive on your phone.

You start flicking through them, and find an image of Monica Davies. You show it to the man. 'Yeah, that's her.'

'Do you know her name?'

'Smith, I think. Went to introduce myself once, and her son said that's what they were called.'

'And you're sure it's her,' you check, as you flick through to try and find another photo just to confirm.

'Definite,' he says as he watches your phone screen. 'And there's her son.'

Your world stops for a minute. 'Which one? Which one's her son?'

You go through the folder of pictures Lambie has sent you slowly. He stops you. 'Him.'

'Definitely?'

'There's nothing wrong with my eyes,' he snaps.

'Sorry. I just needed to be sure. Thank you for your help, Mr...'

'Thomas.'

You message DS Lambie again. It reads simply: 'Get here quickly.' You send the address and go to look at the house again. It took you half an hour to get here, it'll take Lambie the same.

Should you wait this out? Or is it worth having a look around the back, at least?

The clock is ticking – head into the house without waiting by going to **193**.

No, you need to wait for DS Lambie. Head to **205**.

14

The odds are not on your side here. The imposing figure in front of you is leaving only a small gap in the doorway, which you'll need to get through if you're going to escape. You scan Peter Maddock's office for anything that might be of use.

About the sturdiest things within your grasp are the large, bulging ring binders on the shelves opposite the computer. You grab one, sending the others tumbling onto the floor, falling open. Papers start spilling. It seems Peter Maddock wasn't the kind of person who remembers to actually clip the metal bindings shut.

You strike the man in front of you with the ring binder and make at speed for the small gap next to him. As he recoils in pain, he regains his composure just in time – for him, not for you. He flicks his leg out and sends you tumbling. You roar in pain.

It's not the fall that's hurt you, although you've taken a knock on

your way down. No, it's the two open rings on the ring binder that you've landed directly on top of. You look down at your wrist, now impaled on stationery. Not even expensive stationery.

The blood starts gushing out of your wrist. You panic: the bindings must have gone through your artery. You're losing blood, and fast.

The man panics too. He grabs the computer base unit, and yanks it away from the wall. The assorted leads snap out, severing any connection it had. He glances back at you, bleeding out on the floor, and mutters a genuine-sounding 'sorry' as he bounds out of the room.

You look at your arm. Your radial artery, you guess. If the ring binder has cut as deep as you think, you've got less than two minutes for somebody to find you.

Just two minutes.

You never stood a chance.

The case of the new officer in Midsomer is destined to be filed away for all time.

THE END

Go to p.293 to read your performance review.

With Frank Woollaston momentarily distracted, you take your opportunity and head past him towards the kitchen. It doesn't take long for him to regain his composure, and he's after you in a flash. You swing the kitchen door closed with all your strength, but it seems to bounce straight back off his face without affecting him at all. You remember the back door and make a beeline for it.

In your determination to get there as fast as possible, you stumble slightly, narrowly avoiding a rather nice-looking cube-shaped pedal bin. In a stroke of luck, your trailing leg manages to trip Frank Woollaston as you make a lurch for the back door. He loses his balance and starts to fall to the floor. Quick as a flash, you slide the pedal bin towards where you hope Frank is about to fall.

All those years Veronica spent making sure her floor was pristine have been well spent. The bin glides effortlessly across the floor, and Frank Woollaston meets it face first. The expensive chrome finish of the bin admittedly looks a little less like new as a groggy Frank falls down flat on the floor. Taking no chances, you lift the bin and give Frank's face another chance to see it close up just for good measure.

'Call the station,' you shout through to the other room.

'I–is he okay?'

'You might want to get them to send an ambulance. And check if your bin is under warranty,' you add.

The emergency vehicles take a few minutes to arrive. You retrieve your phone from the floor: completely broken, no chance of retrieving anything from that. You keep conversation with Veronica to a minimum. She's going to have plenty of time to tell her part of the story.

Frank Woollaston slowly regains consciousness as the ambulance crew come in. Veronica is led to a police car and read her rights. The Chief Inspector walks in and heads straight towards you. 'I don't quite know how you did it, Detective, but you seem to have solved a mystery I didn't even know we had. I'm assuming it'll only be a matter of time before he cops for the murder of Peter Maddock as well.'

'What about Veronica Woollaston?'

'Well, I suspect she's hiding something, but we'll see what we can get. In the meantime, I think you've earned a good night's rest. And you can take tomorrow off.'

You're not going to do disagree with that. You head back to your hotel and look at the menu for tomorrow's lunch. A nice lunch with a side dish of Plummer's relish, perhaps? What could go wrong with that?

Well done, Detective. It looks like you found the murderer...

THE END

Go to p.293 to read your performance review.

16

'Mr Woollaston,' you say, as calmly as you possibly can. 'I've been expecting you.'

'And I've been watching you, Detective. Didn't expect to see you here, though.'

You shuffle the newspaper in front of you, which is disguising your phone. Muscle memory kicks in, and you try to hide the fact that you're dialling out. All you manage to do is hit the button that redials the last call to your phone. Your eyes don't leave those of the man in front of you, even as you start to feel a thumping sensation in your head.

'I'm arresting you, Mr Woollaston.'

'You're welcome to try, Detective,' he retorts.

You attempt to stand up, and realize you've got a real problem here. You glance at the tea and see what's happened. He's slipped something into it. Presumably he's told the nurse outside that he's happy to carry the drink into the room. That gave him ample opportunity to spike the brew, and also ensures that the medical staff won't be in a rush to return to the room.

It's down to you. You're not sure how much time you have as the poison starts to work its way around your body. The same poison, you assume, that claimed the life of Monica Davies.

A momentary panic. What if your phone can't pick up the conversation properly, among all the beeps and through the newspaper? How are you going to get out of this?

You need to keep him talking, don't you? Head to **19**.
Maybe this is a good time to try and raise the alarm, and call for help? Go to **147**.
Or what about shifting your phone to a better position? That's worth a try, isn't it? You need **217**.

17

There are two reasons why you think it's probably best you sit alongside Veronica Woollaston in her room, as she slowly starts to doze off again. The pain medication she's on is clearly having an effect.

The first is your own safety. For Frank Woollaston to get at you here, he's going to have to come all the way through the hospital to do so. Plus, although Veronica's room is a little isolated from the main ward, you're comforted by the fact that people check in on her from time to time. There's also a button to call for help here.

Secondly, you reason that if there's anywhere Frank Woollaston is likely to appear before he leaves Midsomer, it's here. He's either going to be on the lookout for you, or he's going to have one final confrontation with Veronica. This, you guess, is going to be the venue for that.

You settle down, and after around half an hour you hear light snoozing sounds from the bed next to you. A message flashes up on your phone: the searches at the house in the village of Bunbury have come up with nothing. No further clues at Veronica's home or Peter Maddock's house. It feels all or nothing as you sit here: a final roll of the dice to try to solve the case.

The snoozing sound begins to turn into a snore. You look at your watch and pick up the newspaper. A bit about the competition, a headline about the murders. The rest of the newspaper is testament to the fact that village life just carries on.

The door opens and a nurse pops her head around the corner. 'Do you want a cup of tea?', she asks.

'That's really kind, thank you.'

'Back in a minute with it.'

An article towards the middle of the paper talks of upcoming committee elections due to take place. The world really does keep turning, you think. The door opens again and tea is placed on the table by your side. You're engrossed in the newspaper, so you offer a thank you and keep reading.

You take a sip of the drink. Just what you need, you think.

'That taste good, Detective?'

You look up. The person who brought you the drink wasn't a nurse. There's a man in front of you. Your heart skips a beat as you see Frank Woollaston looking straight at you.

Hit the button at the side of the bed and call for help! Quickly! Go to **162.**

Get Frank talking – see if you can record the conversation and prove he's alive that way. That's at **16.**

18

'Just let me go,' you say. 'I'm not here to get in your way and I just want to leave.'

It's a male voice you don't recognize. The web camera is pointing at him too, but broadcasting to nobody. You're not going to resolve his identity here.

He mulls things over for a second, and simply says, 'Go. Now.'

You don't need a second invitation. You nervously squeeze past and head down the stairs. 'If I don't hear your car driving away in the next three minutes,' he calls after you, 'I'll be coming for you.'

You believe him, and head straight to your vehicle. You call what's happened in to the station, but you reason there's little point. By the time any backup gets here, he'll be long gone – which is indeed what happens. As you make your way to Norton for the final stages of the competition itself, you get word from the uniformed officer on the scene that there's nobody there, just that the computer appears to have been taken.

As you arrive at Norton, lots of threads are swirling around in your head: not least why Veronica and Peter were communicating via computer. Still, you quickly switch your attention back to the competition. Head to **63**.

19

Whatever toxin's going through your system now, it's doing its work fast. You don't have time to waste here. 'I've got the evidence,' you say, your voice weak.

He looks at you, puzzled. 'The murders. We know you committed the murders.'

'You don't know anything, Detective,' he spits back, knocked a little out of his stride.

'I've been sitting here waiting for you, Mr Woollaston. Seeing you in the flesh is the final piece of the jigsaw.'

'It's too late, Detective.'

You cough, your head swimming and your thoughts muddled.

'Mr Frank Woollaston,' you say.

'Yes. What?' he snaps back.

'Thank you.'

As you slump back in your chair and your eyes start to close, you allow the newspaper on your lap to slip down, and reveal the phone that's been broadcasting the conversation. You hope it's caught enough of it, but the last thing you see before your eyelids give up is a look of genuine panic on his face.

When your eyes eventually reopen, you find yourself in a hospital bed yourself, attached to drips and with machines chirping away. You're groggy but still alert enough to see the Chief Inspector sitting next to you.

'How long have I been out?'

He looks at his watch. 'About twenty-three hours. You're very lucky.'

He picks the story up: of how Frank Woollaston panicked and, as he crashed out of the hospital side room, how the nursing staff were alerted and found you quickly. The poison he'd laced your drink with was potent – of amphibian origin – but they got to you in time.

As you take it all in, you ask: 'Frank Woollaston?'

'At the station, facing a growing number of charges, two murders included. He did manage to get away from the hospital, but we were on our way by then. He managed to crash his car as he tried to escape – he wasn't difficult to spot.'

'Veronica?'

'She's being discharged this morning, and then we're taking her to the station too. There are a few charges she's going to face.'

It's quite a story. How Frank Woollaston faked his death for the life insurance money, with help from Peter Maddock and the local amateur dramatics society's stage makeup department. All of the work on those shows wasn't wasted. Then Peter starting to blackmail Veronica when he fell short of a few quid. Veronica, in turn, pushing forward the idea of a suspiciously expensive flower contest when she could no longer meet Peter's demands.

There are still small details to fill in, but the Chief Inspector seems satisfied that the investigation will now be able to get to the bottom of pretty much all of it. The committee will have to be disbanded, of course, and there's precious little chance of another Villages In Bloom competition being organized any time soon.

But Detective: congratulations! You came to Midsomer and were instantly faced with a murder investigation. You've nearly died, and uncovered a two-decades-old secret that pretty much nobody here realized was a secret in the first place. What's more, you've solved your first big case in less than half a week.

As you allow yourself to breathe out and try to take it all in, the Chief Inspector's phone buzzes. He answers, and his voice quickly turns serious. As he ends the brief but clearly important call, he looks across at you.

'We need you up and ready as soon as possible, Detective,' he says as he gets up and puts his coat on. 'We might just have another case coming in...'

THE END

Go to p.293 to read your performance review.

Well, that was quick.

Veronica Woollaston bids you good day as you accept her story, and closes the door to her home, reapplying the bolts on the other side of it.

You turn back to your car, a little puzzled by her reaction, but not wanting to get on the wrong side of influential villagers just hours into your new job.

Unfortunately, it proves to be your first mistake.

Your second isn't too far behind. As you mull over Veronica's reaction, and run through in your head the best way to report back to the Chief Inspector, you fail to hear it.

In truth, though, you've never wondered what noise a yucca tree makes as it flies through the air. Turns out it's a quiet swish. What makes a bit more noise is the impact of its ceramic pot as it hits the head of a human being.

Your head, in this case.

The pot shatters into pieces. You think you can just about see a man's leather glove.

Is it a man? Where did he come from?

You'll never know the answer. The thick trunk of the tree's base is raised behind you. You've always admired a good yucca, but in this instance you have to admit your enthusiasm for the plant is waning.

Your final thought as it suddenly interfaces with your head is that Midsomer CID's interviewing panel will be meeting again a lot sooner than anticipated. The Chief Inspector has got a difficult phone call to make to your next of kin, too...

THE END

Go to p.293 to read your performance review.

21

You stop and ponder what Mrs Woollaston has just told you. Is she telling you the truth, or just trying to get the competition moving, you wonder? Whichever it is, the one thing you're sure of is that the woman in front of you is genuinely upset.

'Mrs Woollaston, if you're being threatened, you really need to report it, to come down to the station and make a statement.'

'I can't. I just can't.'

'Why can't you?'

She looks at you as if she can't believe you've asked the question.

'Because I think someone is trying to kill me, Detective. How do you think they're going to feel if they suddenly see me heading to the station?'

'The same way they'd feel about me being here now?'

'Come on, Detective,' she begs. 'You know there's a difference between someone talking to the police and someone being taken down to the station.'

'That's assuming someone's watching you. Is that what you think?'

'I have no idea. I just know I'm scared.'

That's something you believe. She's clearly not going to budge, though, unless you arrest her. And the truth is you've nothing to arrest her for. It's her decision, and you can't make it for her.

What do you do now? Do you want to try and catch a word with Monica? Find her at **2**.
Or with the competition cancelled, do you want to call it a day and try to mop up what you can tomorrow? Go to **69**.

22

You head out to the back garden and see the footsteps leading up to the fence at the back. You walk past a potato planter flush against the fence and climb over to see what lies behind. A lot of woodland is the answer, but you look to see where the most obvious ways are next. Presumably, whoever it was will have wanted to make a quick getaway. As it turns out, just two minutes sees you come back out onto the main road, walking away from Veronica's house.

You walk past the windmill floral display, the centrepiece of the area's Villages In Bloom entry.

Next, you head back towards Veronica's house and note the small road running alongside it, near where the vehicle you spotted before is parked. Might that be worth a look? Go to **114**.
Or you could go back into the woodland and see if you can spot anything that may have been left behind? That's at **195**.

23

You beckon Veronica inside and identify yourself to the receptionist. They've been expecting you. Once signed in, you're given protective clothing and quickly led deeper into the building.

Veronica composes herself, then follows you in. A distinctive shape lies under a white sheet.

'Ready?' says the surprisingly young coroner, beckoning you in.

You nod. You've done this before, but it never gets easier. This one, too, takes you by surprise.

'W–what's that smell?' Veronica gasps as the cover is taken off the lifeless body. It's a good question. There's something more than the natural aroma of death here.

'Damsons,' says the coroner.

'Damsons?'

'Damsons.'

Both you and Veronica look puzzled. The coroner offers no further information. She's got a more pressing job to attend to.

'Can you confirm that this is Mr Maddock?'

Veronica slowly nods.

'Thank you, Mrs Woollaston,' you say. 'Could you just wait outside a minute?'

As Veronica leaves and closes the door behind her, you take the coroner aside. 'Damsons?'

She looks at you. 'You're new to the area, aren't you?' she smiles.

You smile back. 'That obvious?'

'Mr Maddock was seemingly killed when a metal shelving unit collapsed on top of him,' she explains. 'The shelves were full of his homemade damson jam, which apparently he'd been planning to sell at the festival this weekend. They caught him plumb on the head

– if you'll excuse the pun.'

You try and process what you're being told.

'Are you telling me that Mr Maddock was killed by three dozen jars of damson jam?'

'Four dozen would be my guess,' she says. 'But that's our assumption so far. We've just got a few more things to check before we can confirm that.'

You take out your notepad and scribble down the details. The smell of those damsons punctures the air. You'd felt a little hungry on the drive over, but you might just give your packed lunch a miss.

You thank the coroner for her time and head back to the reception.

It's clear you need to make your way to Little Norton and see the scene of death for yourself. But there's a problem: Veronica Woollaston is nowhere to be seen.

Where could she be?

'If you're looking for the lady you came here with,' the receptionist says, 'she left.'

What now? Head back to Veronica's house to try and find her? Go to **168.**
Time to go and see the murder scene in the village of Little Norton. That's over at **84.**

24

You've got to push this, and young Mr Webber hasn't endeared himself to you.

'The typing on the entry form you submitted is very similar to a threatening note that was received and reported earlier today,' you tell him.

He looks at you, bemused.

'You've got to be kidding me,' he says, affronted. 'You're coming to my front door late at night to accuse me of sending a threatening note?'

'I'm not accusing you of anything Mr Webber,' you argue. 'I'm following up a line of enquiry.'

'It's a bloody typewriter,' he snaps. 'They type. The letters all look the same.'

'Unless the ribbon is starting to fade,' you flatly respond.

'This is unbelievable,' he snarls, his mood starting to turn. 'What exactly do you want from me, Detective?'

'I need to eliminate you from my enquiry,' you say. 'I'd like to see your typewriter, please.'

'It's not my typewriter,' he snaps back.

'Do you have it?'

'Are we done?'

'I need to see that typewriter.'

'Well, you're not coming in here.'

You're hitting a dead end, and Trevor Webber is clearly not minded to cooperate. He wasn't in the best of moods when he opened the door, but he looks positively volcanic now.

You've had enough of this. Call the Chief Inspector and ask if you can search Trevor Webber's house. That's at **86.**

Walk away. It's a loose lead anyway. Maybe head over to see his parents instead? They're at **209.**

25

Sometimes, you've just got to try safety first. You stay absolutely still and silent. You don't notice anything, of course, and you lie under the sturdy old bed as the intruder walks away unchallenged with what could bc crucial evidence. But on the up side, you're able to walk out of the house in one piece.

Your car isn't in one piece when you get to it, though. After checking in with the uniformed officer and letting them know what happened – helpfully, they haven't seen or heard a thing – you get to your vehicle to find that its tyres have been let down.

You call the station and tell them what's happened. The officer stands with you while you wait for someone to collect you, and thankfully it's not long before a police car speeds along the road to do so.

You thank the officer, get in to the car and head to Norton and the competition announcement. You feel bereft of clues and no closer to working out who killed Peter Maddock.

Here's hoping you find one or two things out at the village hall to get this investigation back on track. That's at **63**.

26

Veronica Woollaston looks on with tears in her eyes as you make the call to the station. At first, there's some incredulity on the other end of the line, and you have to repeat yourself. But it doesn't take long for your colleagues to swing into action. You sit with Frank and Veronica as you wait for the police car to come and take them both away.

'Why? Why come back?', you ask him. 'If you've managed to convince Midsomer you're dead for nearly twenty years, why return?'

'I miss her. I love her. I've always loved her.'

The look on Veronica Woollaston's face suggests that it's not quite so straightforward from her perspective. She's steadfastly saying nothing here, though. It's up to him to tell the story.

'Have you been back before?'

'A few times. Let's just say it's very useful that the house over the road has been empty for a while.'

As he tells you the rest of the story, you can't help but feel he's leaving details out. But he knows what he's doing. He's making sure that nothing at all will incriminate Veronica, and ensuring all the blame lands on him.

Do you buy it? It doesn't really matter. He's confessed to the murder of Peter Maddock, even if he's not convincingly explained why he did it. He's given enough details about the faking of his own death. It'll be ample to lock him up for a very long time to come.

It won't stop more questions, of course, but he's going to be careful how he answers them. The rumours and gossip about whether Veronica was involved are likely to continue, but there's nothing anyone can do about that.

The Chief Inspector is certainly a very happy man. As far as he's concerned, you've solved a murder case in a day. And even though you still can't lose those niggling doubts that all's not quite what it seems, as Frank Woollaston is led out of the house in handcuffs and into a police car, you accept that at least some justice has been done here today.

THE END

Go to p.293 to read your performance review.

27

There's no way you're letting these two get their own way. You ask both Monica and Veronica if there's a place the three of you can go to for a conversation. You're led down a corridor to the side of the main hall, and you all end up in a small office.

These two are clearly firm friends. The organizer and deputy organizer of the competition, the chair and deputy chair, too. The two main figures on the committee itself. A pair of women with plenty to say for themselves.

Yet they're both stonily silent.

'You both wanted a word? Does someone want to talk?' you say. You realize that neither was aware that the other had asked for a quiet chat. It feels an agonizingly long silence, one you have no intention of being the first to break. Eventually, it's Veronica that speaks up.

She quickly finds her tempo. It's just what you'd expect to hear. They've put their heart and soul into the competition, the whole area is excited for it. Nothing, you think, that couldn't have been said out in the main hall itself.

You turn to Monica and she quickly follows the same party line.

'We appreciate that you're new and don't really understand the area,' she says. 'But this is what village life is all about. You must let the competition go ahead.'

The two women exchange a look of agreement with what might be called an inquisitive edge.

They're telling you nothing new, though. It's very simple: do you recommend the Villages In Bloom competition goes ahead or not?

Oh, all right! Let it go ahead. That's at **67**.
No. It's cancelled, and you're off to your car. Go to **214**.

28

Satisfied that there's nobody about, and aware that you're about to try and gain entrance to a property without a warrant, you lean into the gate. You put your weight against it and it starts to give way, the wooden panel cracking. You curse under your breath. There's no way you're going to be able to disguise the fact that you've broken your way in now. You've just got to hope you find something.

Early signs aren't promising. The overgrown garden sticks out from the others in the area, where keeping bushes in order seems to be a badge of honour. There's a small shed, but given the state of the grass, a lawnmower is not among its contents.

As you approach the back door of the conservatory at the rear of the house, your hunch about it being empty seems right. You gaze through the glass and see that it's got the very basics inside, nothing more. Carpet, walls and ceiling.

Once again, though, you're stuck on the outside, and you can't easily get a closer look. The door to the conservatory is locked, and no window appears to be open. You can't risk going around to the front of the house and getting in that way. Instead, you edge around to the side of the building and press your face against the window and this time see what looks like... well, like it used to be some kind of living room.

You've already pushed your luck quite far here, and you resign yourself to calling in some support if you want to get inside. But then your blood freezes as you see what looks like a figure inside the house. You stay still and glance again: there's definitely someone in there, even if you can't make out who they are.

Now what? You can't get in – do you hide yourself away and wait for them to come out? Go to **12.**

This is surely the moment where you need some support. Call for it by heading to **101.**

29

Your phone buzzes as you stand waiting outside the small house in Bunbury. The Chief Inspector is going to be after you. You're pretty much out of rope here. You ignore the call for now, and figure you're going to give this another five minutes. Not that anybody appears in that time. Whoever was on their way clearly isn't now: either that, or they're not showing themselves.

The silence is broken by an alert, sent to DS Lambie's phone this time. 'They've done the trace.'

'Who's the phone registered to?'

'It's a pay as you go, so they don't have contract details.'

'Damn.'

'But they do have information on where it's been used.'

Your eyes light up. 'Are they close?'

'Near the hospital.'

'The hospital where Veronica is?'

He nods. 'And there's something else that's been bugging me. That voice. I recognized the voice, and I know where I've heard it.'

'Go on.'

'I know it sounds like I'm going mad – but I swear that was her husband. Frank Woollaston.'

'The dead Frank Woollaston?'

'Well, he didn't sound very dead, did he?'

'You stay here and see if you can get access to the house. I'm going to see Veronica – and find out if she knows her husband is alive.'

'You sure you want to do that? You know the Chief Inspector's been after a word...'

Head over to see the Chief Inspector over at **80.**
Let the station know Frank is alive! Go to **11.**

30

You don't have all the bank statements in front of you, but from what you can see, in the last six months alone payments amounting to around £30,000 have been made to Williams Consulting.

You call back to the station and ask them to run an urgent search on the company to see what you can gleam. Maybe the Companies House records can shed some light?

You turn to DS Lambie. 'How much do you think this competition has cost them all?'

'I dread to think. Don't forget they haven't paid out the prize money yet either. Given the state of these bank accounts, they haven't got the funds to do that.'

'Why did they offer the prize then?'

'Presumably they did have the funds when they came up with the idea.'

'When was that?'

'Think they started talking about it the year before last. Well, knowing that committee, they talked about it for a couple of years before then. But it started happening around 18 months, two years ago. Chances are they'd have had the prize money then.'

Your phone bursts back into life. That was quick. The news on the other end of it is puzzling, though. The company was set up and registered by a Mr F T Woollaston. But when he died, the name changed. The registration address is an accountancy firm some 100 miles away. And the listed director this time is H W O'Brien.

'O'Brien?' you say to DS Lambie. 'Hazel?'

The penny drops. Hazel O'Brien, Monica Davies' neighbour. But how is she linked to all of this? And what does Veronica know about this company?

Go and question Hazel O'Brien at **34.**
Can you get anything from the company's listed accountants, though? Find out at **66.**

31

As you pull up at the church, you see reminders of the flower competition that the weekend was supposed to be all about. Little Norton really is a beautiful part of the world, you think as you drive through. It's just a shame you've not had a chance to enjoy a quieter first weekend in Midsomer.

It doesn't take you long to find the grave of Frank Woollaston. Instinct tells you it's likely to be the best-tended plot in the church's grounds, and you're proven correct. A few beautiful floral tributes are perfectly placed against an elegant headstone. 'In Loving Memory of Frank Bernard Woollaston.' Nice, simple, to the point.

It seems pretty much everything is in order here, and you've had a wasted journey. By all means take a closer look if you want to – or maybe see if the vicar is about and grab a quick word?

If you want to examine the grave a little more, go to **188.**
But if you're off to look for the vicar, head to **172.**

32

As Hazel O'Brien struggles to recall anything that might be of genuine use to you, you go back to what led you here in the first place.

'Tell me about Williams Consulting.'

'You know about that?'

'I know that you're the listed director of a firm that used to be run by Frank Woollaston. How did that come about?'

She takes a breath. She knows this doesn't look good.

'Veronica asked me. Just to keep Frank's business going after he died. I just signed a piece of paper or two for her every now and then, but that's all it was.'

'Is there any reason why Veronica didn't name herself?'

'I don't think she could. Frank had a few businesses go under before, Monica told me once, and he must have put something in her name. She was disqualified for a while from being a director.'

'Didn't you ask about that?'

'Of course I did. But you've met Veronica. She can be very persuasive. And in truth, I wanted to help her as much as I could after she lost Frank.'

'What do you know about the payments?'

'What payments?'

'The £30,000 your company has received from the Committee.'

She looks shocked.

'Please don't go anywhere else,' you say sternly. 'Make sure you remain where I can contact you. I've got a murderer to catch, but you'll have questions to answer later.'

You need to let the station know Frank is alive now. Dial **11**. *Or take the chance to search Veronica's house while she's still in hospital – can you find out more there? Go to* **163**.

33

You leave the bedroom for a minute and head across the compact landing to the bathroom. Lots of houses in Midsomer would have en suites, you assume. Not Monica's. Is she someone – and she's not the only one here – who pretended she had more money than she did?

The bathroom is clean and organized. A shower cubicle rather than a bath, and a sink with just the one toothpaste in a pot to the side. That, and a glass. Presumably where she kept her dentures overnight?

Nothing stands out here, you think, so you head over to see Hazel O'Brien. Hopefully she can shed a bit more light on all of this. Go to **92**.

You hadn't expected to have to return to Green Vale, but as you pull up outside Hazel O'Brien's house, it seems that she at least was certainly expecting you. A warm cup of tea is waiting for you, next to a light blue lever-arch ring binder.

Hazel has left the door open, and she's sitting at her kitchen table. There's a chair waiting for you. You figure you're just going to let her talk. It looks like she's got plenty to get off her chest.

'This can't go on,' she says, her voice trembling with emotion. 'Everything you need is in there.'

You open the binder and start flicking through. This looks like a far more complete financial picture than the one you managed to retrieve from the house in Bunbury. What's more, Hazel O'Brien is clearly willing to explain it all.

'Nobody should have died for this. *Nobody*,' she adds. And she proceeds to tell you the tale.

You sit there, trying to take it all in. How Monica Davies had to keep her own son secret. How she then found herself caught between her son and her best friend when Peter started blackmailing Veronica.

Hazel O'Brien is less interested in explaining what leverage Peter had over Veronica, but given she's in full flow, you don't really want to interrupt.

She tells you about the night at the start of the year when Monica couldn't cope with it anymore, and confided in Hazel about what was happening. Then everyone involved got little threatening notes to keep them quiet.

Hazel agreed to chair the judging for the Villages In Bloom competition for her friend, knowing full well that the result had been pre-ordained. If they could all get through this, then everyone's money problems would be solved, and things could get back to how they should be.

But they'll never go back to how they should be.

'Do you know who murdered Monica Davies and Peter Maddock?' you ask, after she's spent ten minutes telling you this whole story.

'I–I think it's Frank,' she says, clearly very nervous. Nervous, and very frightened. 'Frank Woollaston.'

Wait: dead Frank Woollaston? The man who died decades ago? And he's very much alive?

Get the news to HQ that Frank is alive: head to **11**.
You need to see those notes from Hazel, don't you? Try **109**.

35

You get into your car, your head brimming with questions. Just what have you found yourself in the middle of? There's a murder, a respectable woman who couldn't get away from the coroner's office fast enough, and the final stages of a flower competition, too. From what you've already seen of the area, not a cheap competition either.

Focus, you tell yourself. Easier said than done, though. As you drive towards Norton, you're struck by how the surrounding villages have taken this competition to their hearts. It's beautiful, you think to yourself.

The village of Norton is set to be the hub of activity for the next few days, a place that looks at initial glance to be untouched by time. A few modern trappings give things away, not least the village hall. A relatively new building, it stands proudly to the side of the green at the heart of the village. It's where the committee meets, where the competition is being coordinated from and, for the purposes of right now, where Veronica Woollaston is likely to be.

You park up, head to the building and push the door forward. Off to the sides of the large hall you walk into are a few doors, and a kitchen hatch lies just by the entrance. It's a busy place, and over the weekend it's set to get even busier once the competition gets going.

A rather elderly woman spots you as you walk in. She clearly doesn't recognize you, but that doesn't stop her beaming a welcoming smile.

'Hello,' she says across the hall. 'Are you here with the vol-au-vents?'

'I'm afraid not,' you say, snapping into detective mode. 'I'm looking for Veronica Woollaston.'

'Ah, yes,' the woman says, her smile dropping a little. 'You must be that new police detective.'

'I am.'

'I'm Monica Davies,' she says, introducing herself without making an effort to come over and shake your hand. 'Veronica's been telling me about earlier today. She was really rather shaken.'

'You spoke to her?'

'She contacted me, yes, and we've been chatting since she got here. She needed to get away, I'm afraid.'

'Do you know why?'

'Yes,' says a voice entering the room. You're already very familiar with the register of it.

'Hello again, Mrs Woollaston.'

She owes you an explanation, and to be fair to her, that's exactly what you get. She explains, cautiously, that it all brings back unpleasant memories. She's only been in that building once before. A different coroner back then, but the death of her husband nonetheless triggers very difficult memories. She was grateful to Monica, to the flower competition, that she had something else to focus on for the minute.

She doesn't mention Peter Maddock once, you notice.

One of the side doors opens and around a dozen people spill out into the hall. They've got the look of people who've just been in a meeting that they didn't want to be in. Never has a bunch of people more convincingly worn a 'that could have been an email' face at the same time.

'The representatives from each of the competing villages,' Monica explains, not waiting for you to ask. 'We've got a competition tomorrow, after all.'

'Wait a minute,' you instinctively respond. 'We've got a murder enquiry here. A man has been killed. And you're still planning to have the competition?'

This does not go down well.

'Of course. We can't cancel it now. Not after all the work that's gone in,' Veronica affirms. She's used to getting her own way, clearly.

But can she get her way on this? Shouldn't you be asking for the whole competition to be called off while the murder is investigated? If that's your choice, go to **119**.
Or do you let it go ahead, and see how things play out from here – perhaps the murderer is still around? Recommend the competition continues by heading to **10**.

36

It's risky, but you feel exposed here. As quietly and stealthily as possible, you edge towards the office door. You hear movement downstairs. It sounds as if someone is looking for something as they make their way towards the stairs. That buys you a little bit of time.

You creep across into the other room and look for a hiding spot. Best to stay safe. The only place you can find is under the large double bed that dominates the room. You slip underneath it and tense up as you hear footsteps climbing the stairs.

Surely whoever it is knows you're here?

Apparently not. Either that, or it's not you they're after. Curious, you think. Could it be that the person on the other end of the call might not be the person in your house now? Or that they just wanted to distract you?

From your vantage point, though, all you can see is their feet. Feet that turn left at the top of the stairs and head into the office room.

You see what they're after, as they remove the base unit of the computer and take it. A quick look around and they turn back towards the stairs.

What do you reckon, Detective? Want to try and stop them?
Go to **104**.
Or maybe just edge forward a little and see if you can catch a glimpse of their face? Risky, though... You need **183**.
Nope. Stay still. Let them go. Head to your car. Get out of here. That'd be **25**.

37

The pair of you decide to give the number a try. But you figure that if whoever it is gets a call from an unknown phone, they're unlikely to answer. Or at the least, it'll raise their suspicions.

'Mr Thomas, we need to borrow your phone. We need you to call the number and hand it over to us.'

By this stage, he's worried about being drawn into an investigation he has no urge to be a part of, and complies.

You and DS Lambie hold the phone so that you can both hear. It takes a single ring before it's answered.

'I told you, never call this number,' a male voice snaps.

A look of recognition darts across DS Lambie's face. He muffles his voice as best he can.

'Sorry,' he offers by way of reply. You can hear a car engine and plenty of background noise. Whoever it is, they're on the move.

'Who is it? Who have you seen?'

'A detective,' Lambie coughs.

'Keep them talking. I'm on my way.' The line goes dead.

'We need to get some backup,' you say to DS Lambie. He agrees, but figures you've got a bit of explaining to do when the time comes. At least you didn't break into the house. Nonetheless, he calls through to the station and briefly explains the situation, asking them to run a trace on the number too.

'They've got a couple of uniformed officers closest, they're sending them.'

'What about the number?'

'Running it through the system now. They're going to come back to me.'

You wait around for a bit. At one stage, Mr Thomas tries to go back to his house, but you ask him to stay. Safety in numbers, perhaps, but he's also a little bit wrapped up in this.

'You recognized the voice?', you whisper to DS Lambie.

'I'm not sure,' he says. 'I feel like I should, but...'

He trails off, looking uncertain.

It takes a while for the uniformed officers to arrive; it's some 20 minutes before they pull into the small road. Thing is, they've arrived, but the mystery caller is nowhere to be seen.

Have they been spooked? Did they spot the police presence and give this one a miss?

Give the number another try at **157**.
No, have patience. Sit tight and go to **29**.

As Trevor Webber gets out of his stylish sports car, he spots you approaching.

'Ah, the new detective.'

'Hello, Mr Webber. Cutting it fine, aren't you?'

'Nothing around here ever runs on time, you must have worked that out.'

You're certainly getting a taste of that today. You also suspect that Trevor Webber seems to have his finger on what goes on in the area – among other things.

'One or two people saw you having a bit of a commotion here earlier today. I wondered if I could just ask you a question or two?'

'That'd be that busybody Polly Monk, I suppose.'

'I've not spoken to her about it, actually, but several people did see you having a heated argument. You hardly had your disagreement in private.'

'When it comes to Polly Monk, I'll have a disagreement anywhere. Comes across all innocent, doesn't she? Well, I was just giving her a taste of her own medicine.'

'What medicine would that be?'

'She's another one of those who reckon they just have to turn up to win a competition like this. Looking down at anyone under the age of 50. I was just ribbing. In all honesty, I've been giving grief to anyone associated with this competition all week.'

'Any particular reason?'

'A bit of fun. I think they all need knocking off their perch a bit.'

'Like Peter Maddock was knocked off his perch?'

'I didn't mean it like that. And you know it.'

He's right. You did know it. Still, Trevor Webber strikes you as the kind of man better at dishing things out than taking them.

'You said she comes across all innocent.' He looks puzzled. 'Polly Monk. You said she comes across all innocent.'

'Well, she does.'

'And was that what you were talking to her about?'

'Sort of. There was some attempted sabotage of the displays yesterday, and I wouldn't put it past her to be involved with it.'

Your conversation is interrupted suddenly by a sudden bustle of activity from outside the village hall. It looks like an announcement is finally about to be made. Best make your way over there. *Head to* **145**.

39

There are only a few houses overlooking Peter Maddock's home and garden. You peer around, looking for any signs of life behind their windows. There's barely even a car around here, you realize, save for yours and the police vehicle parked outside the house.

All you can really do is walk along the adjoining road, hoping to spot something. It doesn't take you long to realize this is something of a forlorn exercise. After 15 minutes, you turn and return to the house. As you do so, you notice a car driving away that appears to have someone in police uniform in it. That can't be right, can it?

You dash back towards Peter Maddock's house, and notice that the door is now slightly ajar. Is someone in there, you wonder? But also, what's with the car quietly edging away?

Head back into the house and found out what's gone on there.
Go to **55**.
There's something really odd about that car and you need to follow them. Give chase! *Go to* **71**.

40

The best, most substantive lead we've got at the moment is that house, you reason.

You know that Monica Davies and Peter Maddock met up there. What's more, it'd explain the fact that both of them seemed to be struggling for funds if they were having to pay the upkeep on another property. Given that everyone else on the Midsomer village committee seemed to live in expensive houses, the fact that Monica didn't had already stuck out a little to you.

You turn to DS Lambie. 'What's the quickest way to find out who owns a house around here?'

He thinks for a minute and reaches for his phone. Not much signal, but enough to get a call in. You continue reading the handwritten cards, the brief notes of love between a son and his mother – and vice versa. You struggle to imagine the difficulty of keeping such a secret.

DS Lambie finishes his call. 'Might be a dead end,' he shrugs. 'The house is a rental property. Managed by a company out of the area. The landlord is someone called Troy, but I don't think there's anything in it. Assume they just rented whatever house they could afford.'

'Whose name is it rented under?'

'A false one. Smith.'

'Not much point running a search on that.'

'What's more interesting is how long it's been rented for. At least ten years, according to their records.'

'No records before that?'

'It's a big national company that acquires smaller local firms. The records got muddled. They're searching for us, but I don't hold out much hope.'

'So we're left with a property that Monica Davies and Peter Maddock had for the best part of a decade, and neither is alive to tell us about it.'

'That's about the measure of it.'

DS Lambie's phone buzzes this time. 'It's the Chief Inspector. He wants you back at the station. He's getting fed up with being ignored.'

Run that search for Peter Maddock's birth certificate. Head to **150.**

You need to go and see the boss now. Go to **80.**

41

You head back towards the village hall as Heidi McLeish's car roars away, and make a beeline for Polly Monk. She's on the edge of the crowd, reluctantly accepting congratulations from one or two well-wishers for making the shortlist. Still, she doesn't look all that thrilled, considering how close she and her village are to a £100,000 prize.

'Can we have a word?' you ask.

The two of you walk away from the crowd to try and find a more private spot.

'H–how can I help?' she says, her confident demeanour now notably lacking.

'I see congratulations are in order.'

'Thank you. We'll just see what happens next.'

'Not everyone seems very happy with you being on the shortlist.'

'I presume you mean Heidi. I saw her storm away.'

'The two of you friends?'

'Not really. We're both a little on the outskirts of all this brouhaha usually. But I think most of us were expecting her to win. It's a surprise she's not on the list.'

'Is it?'

You let the question linger in the air.

'It really is,' she insists.

'She doesn't seem as surprised as you, by the looks of it.'

'This whole competition has felt wrong,' she argues. 'Poor Peter Maddock was boasting he was going to win it last week, and look at him now. And then there's Old Norton. What a surprise when Veronica Woollaston's village made it to the final three.'

'From what I understand, most people expected it to be. It was said to be an excellent display.'

'Not when the judges saw it, it wasn't.'

'And just what do you know about that?'

'I hear what people say. Everybody knows that it was sabotaged.'

'True. But not everyone knew that it was sabotaged before the judges could see it.'

'Oh come on, that's just common sense.'

'Maybe. Is there anything else you know about the sabotage?'

'Like what? What else is there to know?'

'Like is this linked, do you think, to the murder of Peter Maddock?'

Suddenly, Polly Monk looks panicked. She's struggling for words. You don't break the silence and let her off the hook. She starts to cry.

'I promise you, Detective, I don't know anything about Peter. I was as shocked as everyone else.'

'What *do* you know about?'

She breaks.

The confession comes. Yes, Polly Monk was fuming at the idea of Veronica Woollaston winning the competition. Yes, she was angry that none of those sycophants – her word – on the committee would stand up to her. And yes, she organized weedkiller to damage the Old Norton display.

'But that's all I did, I promise,' she sobs.

It's one little part of the mystery solved. But do you believe her innocence when it comes to Peter Maddock? You can head back to the commotion at the village hall, by heading to **199***.*
Or you think you've on to something here. Keep questioning Polly Monk. There might be something else. Go to **159***.*

42

You don't think twice. You grab the headset, put it on and answer the call. You've not had time to get your recorder going. Not for the first time, you're on your own here.

'Hello, Detective,' says the voice coming through the earphones. You stare at the screen. Pitch black. They've disguised their voice as well. Why? Is this somebody you've met before, you wonder?

'What do you think you're doing?' the voice says. There's a long pause, and it's clear this conversation will not continue without you giving an answer.

You're on the back foot here, and you know it. 'Who is this?' you ask, keeping your question to the point. 'And how do you know it's me?'

'Mr Maddock has a webcam connected to his computer,' the voice replies.

'But how did you know somebody would be here to answer the call? You must have known that he died yesterday?'

'That's a better question, Detective. I saw you enter the house.'

A chill goes down your spine. You're in danger here. What's more, it's somebody who recognizes you – and you've only been in the area for just over a day. You reach for your phone and try and get a call out for help.

'Don't.'

You keep on reaching, just slower.

'Don't. You will not be told again.'

Blast.

They continue. 'And you didn't answer my question, Detective. What do you think you're doing?'

You find some steel from deep within you.

'I'm investigating Peter Maddock's death,' you reply. 'Would you happen to know anything about that?'

'I know that it's not a good idea for someone to be snooping around the way you are. Not if they know what's good for them.'

'I'm a police detective. It's my job.'

'I'd give this one a miss. Or, let's just say, not try too hard. If you catch my drift.'

'I'm not sure I do.'

'Oh, you're not that naïve. I know it's only your second day, but I don't believe for a second you're missing my point.'

They seem to know a lot about you. Now what do you do?

'But tell me about you,' you say. 'I presume you're whoever X is?'

'You do work quickly, Detective,' the voice says.

'I've seen the messages you sent.'

'So what?'

'I know you were trying to stop Peter Maddock.'

A pause. 'Peter Maddock should have stopped himself. If he hadn't got greedy, then...'

'Then?'

They're rattled. Perhaps a little angry. 'None of this should have happened, Detective. None of it.'

'How was he greedy?', you ask, keeping the conversation on topic.

'You've learned enough from me. I'm asking you, Detective: please leave this alone now. You might not believe this, but I don't want more people to get hurt.'

'You know I can't leave this alone.'

'I really hoped you wouldn't say that,' says the voice, and then the call abruptly disconnects.

They know who you are. They know where you are. And that's when you hear a voice from outside.

Stay inside: you're safer here for the minute. Aren't you?
Go to **122**. *Run downstairs and find out what's happening outside. Go to* **156**.

43

You decide that the typewriter might be something of a red herring here, and instead continue to enjoy the candid, warm company of Geoff Webber. He pours himself a whiskey and offers you one too. You decline, knowing you're on duty and still have to drive back to your hotel. Still, if Geoff Webber wants one, maybe he'll tell you a few more secrets of the area as he enjoys it.

It doesn't take long to steer the conversation onto the village committee. 'My one mistake,' he muses, as he swirls the liquid in his tumbler. 'I'd hoped that committee would be a bedrock of support for people in and around Midsomer. It's been a shame to see its decline.'

He explains that he injected a six-figure sum into its bank account back when it was struggling before. For years, it did what he'd hoped, and gave a bunch of people with too much time on their hands something useful to do. But he's aware of the dwindling financial health of the committee – 'not that they told me directly' – and thinks that the Villages In Bloom competition would have been one last hurrah for it.

'Why didn't you try and stop it? Or intervene with the committee?'

'Because I don't want to, Detective. I've spent forty years building up my businesses, being pulled from pillar to post for twenty hours a day. I actually just want to enjoy my retirement, not to solve everyone else's problems. I've done my bit. If they squandered it and haven't asked for my help since, what do I do?'

You take his point. Still, does he have any further things to look out for? As you get your coat to take your leave, you ask him.

'There's something with Peter Maddock and Veronica Woollaston,' he says. 'She couldn't stand the man. Shut down any conversation when his name was uttered as quickly as possible.'

'Do you think she was involved in his death?'

'I couldn't tell you. That's your job to work out, isn't it? She's never struck me as a murderer, but still, I quite enjoy the safety of living behind a great big gate.'

You thank him for his time and head back to your hotel, your head swimming with thoughts. Tomorrow you can pick up the aftermath of the competition being cancelled, and hopefully make progress with your investigation. Head to **69**.

44

You sit and listen to Polly Monk's story, but it's just not adding up for you. She has no alibi, and has form when it comes to sabotaging the opposition. Presumably, you reason, she tried the same with Peter Maddock. To sabotage him. Maddock had been confident he was going to win the competition, and perhaps Polly Monk needed to make sure he wouldn't.

You work out what must have happened. Sneaking into Little Norton, trying to get some of the weedkiller from Peter Maddock's greenhouse. And then, what, he disturbed her, and she pushed the shelves of damson jam on to him?

You get no sense that she's a murderer, but it seems entirely plausible to you that she went too far and accidentally killed Maddock when she was disturbed. She'd have just meant to hurt him, but it all went tragically wrong.

'I need a car,' you tell the station as you call ahead.

Polly Monk looks confused.

'Polly Monk, I'm arresting you for the murder of Peter Maddock.' You read her rights, and add that a further charge will be levelled against her for the sabotage too.

She looks shellshocked as she's driven away.

It seems open and shut, this.

Still, the questioning of Polly Monk back at the station doesn't take long. She's called in her lawyer, but in truth she doesn't really need one. Even the officer at the booking-in desk tells you she thinks this is a bit thin. It takes Polly Monk's lawyer barely two hours to secure her release.

The Chief Inspector is furious. 'What on earth did you think you were doing?' he barks as Polly leaves the station. There's plenty of traffic outside as people leave the long-since-finished competition.

He's not impressed. 'Did you just point the finger at the first person who admitted doing something wrong? What on earth made you think she was a murderer? Barely any motive, not a scrap of evidence and whoever did kill Peter Maddock has now got a valuable few extra hours to make their escape. Well done, Detective,' he says, sarcastically. 'I think we'll keep you to desk duty in the future.'

Gulp.

Better luck on your next case, Detective. If you're ever allowed another. This one really hasn't worked out at all.

THE END

Go to p.293 to read your performance review.

45

You need to keep the momentum with you here, you figure. There's little point in waiting for them to come to you: they're already at something of an advantage. You just need to charge past and get out.

You take a few steps back from the door, as you barely make out the sound of someone creeping along behind it. You count down in your head – three, two, one – then gather all the strength you can muster as you blast into it. The door stands little chance and quickly gives way against the force of your shoulder. You take the figure behind it by surprise as you smash it down, the door forcing them back and leaving them flat on the floor.

You swear you see the glint of some kind of weapon in their hand and don't stop to think twice. You can't make out who they are from under the door, but survival and escape are your clear priorities here. You don't lessen your pace as you run towards the end of a small corridor and see an open door just off to the right.

At the end of it there's a further door with an emergency exit sign above it. That one is slightly ajar too, and you race through it to the relative safety of outside.

You take in a blast of fresh air and allow yourself to slow down for a few seconds. You quickly reverse that decision when you hear a clatter from back inside the church.

Whoever was lying under that door is clearly trying to scramble back to their feet. You can easily make it to your car and escape, you figure, and head back to the village hall. If you want to do that, turn to **199***.*

But do you want to be a hero and face down whoever's about to come out of that church? If so, this is your moment. This is what you've trained for. Go to **62***.*

46

You're reluctant to change the subject now that Veronica is actually being more open with you.

'I don't know why, Mrs Woollaston, but your late husband's name has cropped up during this investigation. Was there anything suspicious about his own death?'

She takes a deep breath. 'It was difficult,' she concedes. 'He always tried to busy himself helping people round Midsomer. Lovely Frank, helpful Frank, butter wouldn't melt Frank. First to buy a drink, mowing people's lawns for them, running the local theatre group, that sort of thing.'

'And it was the lawnmower...'

'That killed him? Yes. Another of his purchases we couldn't afford. One of those sit-on mowers that he could show off on. Just an excuse to go round to people's houses, I always thought.'

'Was he violent to you?'

She has to think about her answer.

'He always tried to protect me. Honestly, in those early years I felt so special. If anybody was unkind to me, he was the first to fight back.'

'But?'

'But he had another side to him. When he died I was broken, but also...'

'Also what?'

'Relieved,' she admits. 'Relieved. Not having to wonder who he was with. What he was spending money on now.'

You try and take all this in. The woman with the seemingly perfect life, but when you peel back the layers... the thought suddenly hits you. Could *she* have killed him? You work through this. She's certainly got a motive. Plus, when he died, she benefitted from the policy payout.

She certainly didn't have to worry about money – well, until recently.

You notice a call coming in from the Chief Inspector. You need to go back to the station. But you've still got time for another question here.

Ask Veronica about her money troubles? Try that at **179**.
Was she involved with Frank's death? Pose that question at **216**.

47

You head for your car and take the already-familiar journey to Veronica Woollaston's expansive home. It takes her some time, understandably, to answer the door. Your watch confirms it's just gone midnight, and she arrives at the door wearing a dressing gown and a rather unimpressed look.

Not unreasonably, she wants to know what you're doing on her doorstep at this time of night, so you figure you've little choice but to come clean: you believe there's a threat to her safety. She scoffs at the idea, and turns to go back to bed.

'Why was Peter Maddock threatening you, Mrs Woollaston?' you ask as she moves to shut the front door.

It's a swing, you figure. You don't know for certain he was. You've only got one unknown person making the allegation. And yet the way she pauses and gradually turns around again tells you that it's true.

She stares at you mournfully for a few seconds, but it feels like longer. 'You'd better come in,' she says, sadly.

You follow her into the house, to her living room. You sit in the same chair where this whole adventure started less than 24 hours earlier. She goes to the sideboard and pours two drinks, not checking to see if you want one. The crystal tumblers she brings over clearly weren't bought in a sale.

'Was he?' you ask, as she sits herself down and takes a sizeable gulp from her glass.

'Yes,' she admits, the façade of formality and order draining from her face.

'Why?'

'Because he wanted money. He was blackmailing me,' she tells you.

'From the competition?'

'He didn't care how he got it. He just said he needed money.'

You ponder this for a minute, and then go to the elephant in the room. 'What information did he have on you to blackmail you in the first place? Why didn't you report it? What am I missing here?'

'Me,' says a different voice from behind you. 'You're missing me, Detective.'

Uh-oh. What do you do? Have you been led down a blind alley here? Is this the end? Do you try and make a run for it?
Head to **133.**
Or do you stick this out and find out who's behind you?
Go to **89.**

48

'Hello, sir,' you say as you answer the call.

'I'll get to the point, Detective,' he responds, in a very to-the-point manner. 'I've got footage here of you breaking into a house in Bunbury.'

That was quick.

'Yes sir. I was following up an urgent lead.'

'I think it's time you came in for that chat, Detective,' he says. The tone of his voice suggests it's not going to be a very happy one.

Uh-oh.

Go and see the Chief Inspector now: head to **80**.
Ask him for just a bit more time by going to **211**.

49

'How did you find Veronica after Frank died?'

'I can't say I took to her as well as some of the others, but I think you've probably guessed that.'

'It did come across,' you smile.

'She can be a very difficult woman. I appreciate she's had some awful times, but even so, the way they gradually let her have her own way more and more? Well, look where it's got them. Alone, never happy, left missing a man she barely had a nice word about when he was alive.'

'What do you mean?'

'They rowed a lot. Got quite loud once and one of the neighbours called us over. Lots of screaming at each other.'

'What about?'

'Nothing really. They calmed down soon enough, but it never struck me as a very happy marriage. Not that you'd know it from the way she tends to his grave. If you ask me, she's nicer to him now he's gone than she ever was when he was alive.'

'I take it he's buried in the area?'

'At the church down the road from Veronica's. Once a week you'll find her down there, changing his flowers and tidying it all up. The proper grieving widow.'

'You don't think she killed him or anything, do you?'

'No, nothing like that. She's two-faced, but she's no killer. I'd like to think she just regrets the way she treated him. Maybe he'd have regretted the way he treated her. But I wouldn't bet on it.'

You thank Shirley Ambrose for her time, and get up to leave. 'Good luck with this one, Detective,' she says. 'I heard about poor Peter. Do let me know if there's anything I can do.'

You promise you will and head back to your car. But what now? Is it time to go back to Norton and whatever's left of the Villages In Bloom competition? Go to **199**.
Or perhaps you should swing by Little Norton on the way, and take a look at this grave. You never know. Go to **31**.

50

In truth, you'd rather not be doing this bit yourself, but as you drive to Norton and its village hall to confront the committee, you figure this is the way it's got to be.

You ring ahead to alert them you're on your way and that you need to see them all: the six women who seem to pull the strings around Midsomer and its committee. You've met Veronica already, of course, and Monica. You recall the other names: Deirdre Foot, Susanna Swann, Patricia Moore and Doreen Webber. You're surprised, though, to see that two of the committee aren't present when you arrive.

It's Veronica who spots you first and tells you. 'I'm sorry, it's just me, Monica, Patricia and dear Deirdre here at the moment. Will we do?'

'Not really,' you say. 'I was clear I needed to see you all. Where are the other two?'

Veronica looks a little put out, but then regathers her composure. 'I can try and get hold of them for you. Who was it you wanted to talk to?'

'All of you together, ideally.'

'Well, as you can see, we're all a bit spread out. Can we do it after the competition? We're expecting the judges back soon, and we're running a bit short on time.'

You call the station and explain the problem. It looks like there's two women you need to talk to urgently, who are in different parts of the area. Can you have some support?

No, you can't. Lambie's out of action, and every other officer on duty is involved in the competition or working on the murder case. Worried as to who might know that Lambie has been asking about the committee, you decide to play things close to your chest, which means that you're going to get time to talk to just one of these women before the competition enters its final stages.

Take your pick, Detective. Who's it going to be?
For Susanna Swann, the committee secretary, head to **164**.
Or how about Doreen Webber, its longest-serving member?
Go to **59**.

51

You take in what Monica has just told you. This isn't just a Villages In Bloom competition to drum up a bit of publicity for the area. There's a lot of money at stake here.

Come to think of it, why does a flower show like this have prize money anyway? Isn't a competition like this more a prestige thing? You could understand a cup being presented and a picture in the paper. But £100,000? Just what kind of competition is this?

That thought swirls in your mind as you make your way back to the main hall. There, representatives from the various villages are milling around as you come back in through the main entrance. Veronica is absent. Perhaps she's gone into one of the back rooms.

You approach the group of people congregating around the service hatch, alternating between sipping tea and putting the world to rights. Or, more to the point, putting your decision to halt the competition to rights.

They fall silent as you approach.

'Good afternoon. I didn't get a chance to introduce myself properly.' You hold up your identification card and give a brief explanation of your day so far. Does anyone have any information, you ask?

Well, if they do, nobody's saying. A few feet shuffle, one or two people take an extra sip of tea. Nobody's in a hurry to make eye contact.

'Well, if you do,' you sigh, 'then please contact the station. I'm sure you all know the number.'

One of them asks what they're all thinking. Is there really no way the competition can go ahead? It's your last chance to decide.

It's definitely not happening! Head to your car at **214**.
Maybe they're right. This has to go ahead. Jump to **67**.

52

Veronica had given the odd hint that she may be in danger, but you're not sure you ever fully believed it. Something has gone very wrong, you think, as you look at her.

She's groggy, weary and apparently appears to have fought off the intruder.

Instantly, though, that doesn't ring true to you. Veronica Woollaston is many things, you think, but someone capable of physically defending herself? It just doesn't wash.

Her eyes show no sign of being pleased you're there.

You jump straight to it: 'Who else was in your house, Mrs Woollaston?'

She looks puzzled and shrugs.

'Who was in your house to save you from the attacker?'

That's quite a leap, and a real gamble. But you're working on a hunch here. It's not a hunch she's pleased to hear, either. Tears form in her eyes, and she closes them. The beeping of the machines intensifies, and the doctor alongside her tells you that you're going to have to leave.

As you and DS Lambie exit the building, your phones buzz. The message you read bursts you back into life. 'I'll meet you there,' Lambie says, as the pair of you run to your respective cars and get moving.

Get to Monica Davies' house – and fast. That's at **117**.

53

The beautiful village of Church Fields is the backdrop to your visit to Polly Monk. Her house isn't the easiest to find, on a small road off the main square. But at least Polly seems relatively warm towards you when you knock on the door.

She answers quickly and invites you inside one breath later. Keen to make conversation, you congratulate her on the beautiful floral arrangements in the village.

'Bit bittersweet, but thank you,' she smiles. She offers a drink, which you decline, and the pair of you sit down in her living room.

'I'm sorry the competition is being called off.'

'Well, that doesn't help, obviously. But we never stood a chance anyway.'

'Why? I've not seen many displays as good as the one here.'

'I'm not a betting woman, Detective, but if I were, I would gamble my home, my car and my best cardigan on Old Norton winning.'

'Old Norton?'

'You must know it. It's Veronica Woollaston country. She rules that village and she rules that committee with an iron fist.'

'I know it,' you reply, enjoying the free, speak-your-mind approach of the woman opposite you.

'On the one hand you had Peter Maddock loudly telling everyone he was going to win. On the other, you've got her, who everyone expects to win… is that what you came here to talk about?'

She's been so entertaining, you almost forgot the reason yourself. 'No, I just wondered if you have a typewriter.'

'Over there,' she nods, pointing to a desk in the next room. 'Why do you ask?'

'Just ruling people out.'

She looks puzzled.

'Somebody received a note, and I'm trying to find out who might have written it.'

'A typewritten note? Like the one I sent to Monica?'

You stop and pull the note out of your pocket.

'This one?'

'Yes, that one. Asking Monica to make sure the competition went ahead. Someone was bound to try and cancel it. Is it a problem?'

'Well, it seems a little threatening, to be honest with you.'

'Does it? That wasn't the intention. Monica was the only one any of us could get through to on that committee. I'm sorry if I've caused any problems… hang on, wait a minute.'

She heads to the phone and makes a quick call. She puts in on speaker so you can hear, and her story stacks up. An audibly relieved

Monica Davies is on the other side of the line, and the pair of them chat away happily for five minutes before promising to catch up for a coffee when all this is over.

You see eccentricity in Polly Monk, but little more than that. As you drive away from Church Fields, it's getting dark. You decide to head to the hotel you're staying at and call it a night.

Go to **69**.

'Hang on, hang on,' you say, raising your voice. 'Are you telling me that you're Peter Maddock's mother? And you never thought to mention it?'

Monica backtracks and realizes her predicament. The grief of losing her child to a damson-scented murder. The broken friendship in front of her. The evidence she's withheld.

Her tone softens, but the daggers in her eyes don't. 'He was my son, Detective. Because of the gossips and backstabbers of this village, we had to keep that a secret. His life would have been unbearable otherwise. And now...' she breaks down and sobs. 'I want to know who killed him.'

Veronica's looking shocked, not sure how to react. 'He was blackmailing me, Monica,' she says, struggling to keep any kind of composure. 'He's been blackmailing me for years.'

'Why?' you ask, deliberately keeping your question short to give her as little wiggle room as possible.

She stays silent.

'Because of Frank,' Monica says. 'You may as well tell them now,

Veronica. I can't lose any more than I have. And you're out of options too, aren't you?'

Silence. You're determined to let one of them break it.

'He's alive, Detective. Frank Woollaston is alive,' Monica says. 'Peter helped stage his death. And she had all the benefits: the money, the status. It's Peter who lost everything.'

The Chief Inspector has walked in as all this is being said. He looks as shocked as you.

'Where is he?' the Chief Inspector demands.

'He was here earlier,' Veronica cries. 'But he'll be gone now. He won't be back.'

The Chief Inspector calls for help and asks the uniformed officers to arrest the pair of them. They're led out back past the crowd, one final show for a Villages In Bloom competition that Midsomer will never forget.

Both of them will face charges and maybe even serve time. Frank Woollaston will never be seen again. The Chief Inspector will commend you for your first investigation – even if there are still a few loose ends.

As the last attendees of the Midsomer Villages In Bloom festival finally depart, much the worse for wear courtesy of the local home brew, one turns to the other. 'They promised a weekend to remember, and they weren't bloody kidding...'

THE END

Go to p.293 to read your performance review.

55

Quickly, you head back into Peter Maddock's house. Nothing seems to have been distributed downstairs at least, you quickly gauge. Heading upstairs? Well, it's a different story. Your eyes are immediately drawn to the computer desk and its disarray.

'Oh no,' you exhale.

Oh yes. Gone. Well, that's not strictly true. The screen is still there, and a spaghetti of cables is strewn across the desk. But the computer's base unit has gone. From what you can tell, that's all that's been taken – but what else did they need? Whoever Peter Maddock was communicating with, your best clue seems to have gone.

Resigned, you slump down the stairs and head back to your car. No point giving chase now. Whoever it was is long gone, and the computer too. With no further clues here, you have little choice but to head back to Norton for the competition result.

You check your watch. You're going to have to put your foot down. Can you make it to Norton in just ten minutes?

Spoiler: no, you can't.

It's not that the car couldn't do it, with a fair wind and clear roads. It's not like you're unfamiliar with the route now, either.

No, it's two different factors that are stopping you.

The first is that the tyres on your car have been let down. It's going nowhere for the time being.

The second is the thump on the back of your head that knocks you out cold while you're examining them. It was an unorthodox weapon that took you out: a couple of wine bottles from a wheelbarrow outside Peter Maddock's house. Thankfully, they couldn't do too much damage. It just delayed you, and as you'll learn a little later, it was enough to keep you out of action for the rest of the day.

As you finally come around the following afternoon, the Midsomer Villages In Bloom competition has been completed. A triumph for the village of Old Norton. People have drifted away and gone back to normal lives. And a whole host of mysteries will just have to remain unsolved.

Bad luck, Detective. Sadly, your journey ends here. It's surprising, the amount of damage a good vintage can do.

THE END

Go to p.293 to read your performance review.

You click on Monica Davies' name and the computer whirs into action. It dials, and you recognize Monica's face as it appears on the monitor in front of you. She's on her mobile, it seems, and she's looking puzzled.

The audio is still going through the headset, so you can't hear what she's saying. But she seems to be mouthing a name. Peter.

You watch the screen. 'Is that you?' she appears to mouth.

You flick the screen off quickly as you hear footsteps coming up the stairs. The webcam remains pointed at the door: she can see what's happening, but the mystery figure, you hope, doesn't know they're being watched.

With an invisible witness to events, you're surprised how confident you now feel. The first thing you notice about the figure is that whoever it is, they're wearing a police uniform with a hood. Their shape doesn't match that of the officer outside. You suspect you're not actually looking at a real police officer, but someone wearing a useful disguise. It's something about their manner.

'Who are you,' you bark, 'and what are you doing in this house?'

A male voice responds. 'I don't want to hurt you,' he says. 'I just need the computer.'

'Who are you?'

'Nobody you know, Detective.'

Well, it's somebody who appears to know you're a detective, for a start.

'I'm not moving until you take that hood off,' you say, as you gesture towards the garment disguising their identity.

'I just need the computer.'

'This computer?' you respond, as you look at the aged machine on the desk next to you.

He lurches forward.

'I wouldn't do that.'

'I don't want to hurt you.'

'Then don't hurt me. Who are you?'

He steps forward, and then stops in his tracks. He curses under his breath.

He's spotted the tiny light on the bottom of the camera. He's realized this is being recorded. You watch as his eyes dart to it, and then back to you.

'There's no point disconnecting it now,' you say. 'The last two minutes has been broadcast.'

You pull the headset out of the headphone socket, and the computer speakers crackle into life.

'Who to?' he asks nervously.

'I–I don't believe it.' Monica Davies' voice trickles out of them.

You might not recognize the voice. But Monica certainly does.

'I'll explain later,' he says, directing his comment at Monica rather than you. 'First, I have to deal with the Detective.'

Hang on – this isn't going well.

As the figure approaches, you've got a split second to decide what you want to do.

If you want to try and make a run for it, go to **14**.
Or do you stick this out and try to get to the bottom of what's happening? Go to **60**.

57

Veronica catches your eye as you head back towards the Village Hall. She's seen you disappear, and has the look of a woman trying to regain control of a situation.

'Is she okay?'

'Is who okay?'

'I presume you went after Heidi.'

'No, I came here. She didn't seem very impressed with the shortlist, though.'

'Sour grapes, I'd imagine,' Veronica says. 'I think she believed some of her own hype.'

'What hype is that?'

'Well, people have been telling her for weeks that she's going to win. It must be so disappointing for her to not even make the shortlist.'

Is she gloating? Or is she hiding upset of her own?

'Your village made it to the final, I note.'

'I can't take credit for that, Detective. I'm neutral.'

Yeah, right.

'You didn't look too comfortable on that stage just before,' you say.

'There have been a few reports of loud arguments.'

'Just the to and fro of a stressful event like this, Detective.'

'Care to tell me what the arguments were about?'

'Not really.'

'Something's not right here, Mrs Woollaston,' you say. 'I think it's to do with money. I'll be trying to get hold of the committee's finances to find out more about this competition.'

'You do that,' she says, defiantly. 'You've waltzed into this village with not a care as to how everything works. Now excuse me. I need to get ready for the final announcement. There's much to prepare for it.'

She marches away and, short of arresting her, you can't really stop her. You've got a little bit of time before the final announcement.

Do you hang around for it? It's over at **199**.
Or do you fancy going back to the station to dig into Veronica's background a little more? That's at **5**.

58

You decide to front this out and make it look as formal as possible, so you head out the front of the house. It's a simple latch lock, and as you open the door you call out to your colleague: 'Over here, there's something you need to see.'

It works, for the moment. Mr Thomas pauses. DS Lambie sprints over and walks into the lounge. You close the door behind you.

'What is it?' he asks, looking worried.

'Nothing in here, I just wanted to get you away from him. He's been filming and taking photos. Can't tell if he's been sending them to someone.'

'You think he's linked to all of this somehow?'

'Only loosely, but I know we're pushing our luck staying in this house without probable cause or a warrant.'

'That much is true. Did you find anything?'

'A stack of greetings cards. I've slipped them in my pocket, but we need to go somewhere else to take a look.'

'I'd suggest quite quickly too.'

'Agreed.'

The pair of you exit the house, closing the door behind you. You bid a puzzled-looking Mr Thomas farewell and hope there won't be ramifications there. You follow DS Lambie as he pulls out first, and he drives for a few minutes, then parks up at a small layby alongside a long, quiet road.

You head over to his car and take the small collection of cards out of your pocket – just as a call comes in that the Chief Inspector wants to talk to you urgently.

Do you answer his call? That's **110.**
Or sort through the cards first? Go to **124.**

59

Doreen Webber is just putting her coat on as you arrive at her home in North Castle. 'You don't mind giving me a lift over to the village hall, do you, dear? I don't drive much these days, I'm afraid.'

You hold the passenger door open for her and get into the driver's seat. As you drive off, it doesn't take long for you to discover that Doreen Webber is not a happy lady.

'I'm very fond of Veronica Woollaston,' she tells you. 'What that poor woman has had to put up with I wouldn't wish on anyone. But this whole competition should never have happened.'

'Not a fan?'

'Not a fan. But I want to support Veronica. Monica too.'

'Friends seem important to you?'

'Very much so,' Doreen smiles.

'What about family? Is yours local?'

'You may have met some of them. My grandson, Trevor, is taking part in the competition. My son and daughter-in-law, Geoff and Alice, are paying for it.'

'Deep pockets?' you ask.

'Why yes, dear. You must have learned they've funded the committee and its activities for many years now. Not any more after this, though. The way they've burned through all that money.'

'Who?'

'The committee. There were six figures in the bank just a few years ago. Now where's it all gone? You're not telling me this competition needed to cost anywhere near as much as it did.'

She's got a point. There are enormous sums being banded around here, beyond the prize money itself.

'The competition doesn't do anybody any harm, though, does it?' you ask, seeing if this goes anywhere.

'Tell Peter Maddock that. He'd still be alive if it wasn't for Midsomer Villages In Bloom,' she suddenly sobs. 'And my family's legacy would still be intact.'

Why would he be alive? Ask that at **196.**
That family legacy: query that at **111.**

60

'How do you two know each other?' you say, trying to get some kind of control over the situation.

'Don't hurt the detective,' says Monica sternly. Will her words have any sway? Seemingly so.

'I think you should stay out of it,' he says, directing his words at Monica.

'I don't think you're in any position to negotiate any more. My computer records these calls.'

He pauses for a second and considers his options.

'The detectives of Midsomer have certainly changed,' he says, looking at you and figuring out his next move. 'Shirley Ambrose's generation has long gone.'

'Ambrose?' Monica isn't interested in where this conversation is going. 'Just go, and leave the detective. I think I'm going to go away for a bit now, and I suggest you do the same.'

You still can't see his face, but you can see the panic in his eyes. He turns. You got to follow him, but Monica's voice behind you stops you. 'Don't, Detective. Not by yourself. I'll be sending the recording later. That'll give you what you need.'

'I've got questions for you.'

'I'm sure. But I think it's worth getting this competition done and dusted, don't you?'

Track down whoever Shirley Ambrose is. That's **116.**
Get to the announcement at the village hall. It's at **63.**

61

As you hear the yelp, instinct kicks in and you dash around to the front of the hotel. You scan the car park, looking for DC Turner. It doesn't take too long to spot her, deep in argument by the steps of the hotel.

Breathlessly, you run up to her. 'What is it? Have you got them?'

'Nothing here,' she says. 'Just sorting out someone trying to get into their car when they shouldn't.'

You look puzzled.

'Think they've had a few too many sherbets at the bar. We had a little disagreement. They've gone back inside to get a good night's sleep.'

The receptionist stands at the door. 'Thanks so much for your help,' they say.

DC Turner turns to you. 'Did you find who you were looking for?'

'No. I heard the noise at the front and thought it was them.'

The two of you look at each other, your faces dropping. The sound of a car purring down the road doesn't help.

'I'd best follow whoever that is just in case, but I'm afraid it's likely just to be a passing car.' She heads to her vehicle and speeds away. You retreat to your hotel room and hope for good news, but it doesn't come. If anyone was about and planning to meet you, they're long gone.

All you can do now is head to bed and start again in the morning. Head to **69**.

62

You make the brave choice, even if you feel anything but. The only advantage you had in your last encounter with the mysterious figure was surprise. They're clearly bigger and bulkier than you, and you don't fancy your chances if you can't get the upper hand somehow.

But where? The open graveyard is so well kept, it's hard to find anywhere to hide.

Your eyes dart from side to side as you try and find something, anything. It's no use. The best you've got here is the pair of old trees just by the wall of the church, but they're too far away. Even the wall itself isn't very tall. There's a spade over by the wall, you think, presumably one the gravediggers have left behind. But that's your lot.

It's too late anyway. The little door is flung back open, and you're out in the open, exposed, as the figure comes towards you.

'I thought you'd end up here,' says a voice you don't recognize. 'You're too clever for your own good, Detective.'

'I'm not sure I follow you. Who are you?'

They remove their head gear. In front of you stands a man in his late fifties or early sixties, you'd guess. You've not met, but you certainly feel like you've seen him before.

But where?

'Can't put the pieces together, Detective?'

He walks towards you, closing the gap to just a few metres. Which is when it hits you. You know where you've seen his face before. You know who it is. You might just have found the missing part of the mystery.

But you might also be about to die.

This is no use, you figure. You know who it is now. You need to escape with the information. Make a run for it. *Go to* **91**.
Say his name and see what happens. *Go to* **131**.

63

As you head towards the village hall at Norton, you're relieved that proceedings are running a little late and you haven't missed the start. It gives you some time to explore the green outside, which is now bustling with little stalls as villagers sell their wares.

An empty table stands where Peter Maddock was supposed to be offering his jam. His demise doesn't seem to have put others off, though, with around two dozen tables dotted around selling assorted produce. No shortage of dairy products, for a start.

You walk around and take a look, but more importantly keep your ears open. The death of Peter Maddock is part of the chitter chatter as you'd expect. But there also seems to be some unhappiness about the competition itself. Why is it running late? You check your watch: proceedings in the hall were supposed to have started 45 minutes ago.

From what you can glean, the judges arrived back from their journey around the competing villages pretty much on time, yet they've been locked in a room ever since. One or two people say they've heard raised voices coming from the hall, but you can't tell whether that's true or just people exaggerating a story.

What's certainly clear is that this isn't quite the celebratory event that had been hoped for. On the plus side for stallholders, however, business appears brisk.

You head towards the village hall and find the doors firmly shut. A small stage has been erected outside and the place seems awash with bunting. All homemade, you assume.

You edge towards the hall and see if you can catch any sign of life inside. 'Looking for something?' asks the Chief Inspector as he sidles up alongside you.

'Sorry, sir. I was just trying to find out what the delay was.'

MIDSOMER VILLAGES
IN BLOOM

'You don't know the committee very well. Never take ten minutes to do something when thirty will do.'

'Surely all they've got to do is announce a winner?'

'Not quite. They announce the shortlist of three before they do that. The winner is announced last thing this evening.'

'They like to string it out! Any more leads on who killed Maddock?'

'I was going to ask you that question,' he replies. You bring each other up to speed with what's been going on, but you're still some way short of the breakthrough you need. As you talk, the Chief Inspector spots someone he knows making their way into the hall.

'Tell them to get a move on.'

'I have. They still don't have all the village representatives here, and they don't want to start without them.'

'Who's missing?'

'Trevor Webber.'

Odd, you think.

'Probably off with his latest girlfriend,' the Chief Inspector remarks. 'Bit of a womanizer is young Webber.'

Use the time to go and have a look around the stalls – you never know, you might find Trevor. Do that at **177**.
Or is it worth trying to get into the hall? That's over at **73**.

64

You quickly explain the problem to DS Lambie. He looks over at Mr Thomas and sighs. He doesn't look happy, but does understand the urgency of the enquiry.

'There's nothing to stop us going around the back for a look,' he reasons. 'Best try the front door first.'

'Wouldn't get your hopes up there. According to our friend over there, nobody's been near the house for a little while.'

'We've at least got to go through the motions.' He's got a point. You knock the door and, predictably, absolutely nothing happens. Nobody's in, and the door is firmly locked.

'He's filming us.'

'I saw. Let's give him something to film.'

DS Lambie knocks the door loudly, and says 'Police, please come to the door.'

Nothing, but then it's a bit for show anyway. 'We're coming around the back,' he shouts, wanting to give the impression of doing things properly. Still, it's a look that doesn't hold much water when the pair of you have to clamber over the gate to the side of the house.

The overgrown garden that greets you pretty much reflects the state of the front of the house. You head towards the back door. To your collective surprise, it's barely locked. Possibly not deliberately: the door seems old and looks like it's hanging on by the tips of its fingernails. The two of you look at each other and head inside.

It's not an entirely empty house that you find. In fact, if anything, it looks sporadically lived in. The back door leads in through the kitchen and you head to the kettle to press your hand against it. It doesn't feel warm. If someone's been in here, it wasn't recently. Say what you like about Mr Thomas outside, but he's not misleading you.

'I'm not comfortable being in here,' says DS Lambie. 'We need to get out really. We're going to get in trouble if there's nothing suspicious in here.' You run upstairs and grab a bunch of bank statements you find in a small study room, then the pair of you make a hasty retreat and drive off, meeting again by the side of the road a few minutes later.

Your phone is desperately trying to get your attention, with a no-doubt-unhappy Chief Inspector on the other end of it.

Do you answer it? Go to **110.**
Or do you focus on the bank statements for the minute?
That's **208.**

65

Since time is hardly on your side here, you quickly head around Monica's house. In her living room you're drawn to the cards on the side – birthday cards. And there might just be a clue among them: a card simply signed 'Happy birthday. All my love. P.'

Who could have sent that? No idea. You scurry around, looking for anything else. An address book, a stash of old letters, anything that could give you an insight into who might be behind the card Monica received.

There's a small desk set to the side of the living room. You put on some gloves to ensure you don't contaminate the scene and sit yourself down. You pull at one of the two drawers built into it. A collection of pens and pencils, a few postage stamps, a couple of local membership cards.

The second drawer doesn't have any kind of correspondence archive, but there is an address book. Beautifully presented handwritten entries, and most pages full of names, addresses and phone numbers. You flick to P, but nothing stands out. Frustrated, you flick through the rest of the book, as you hear the scene-of-crime team move in and start ushering you out of the room.

You turn to the back of the book and notice that the Z pages have just one listing. Curiously, not a listing with a name on it, either.

Just an address. Not even a full address: a postcode and a house number. You snap a picture of it on your phone and leave the room, inputting the postcode into your map application.

It leads to an address around half an hour away in the village of Bunbury. But what could be there? Follow that up at **13.** *Or is this where you head over to Veronica's house. Two crimes have been committed here – maybe there's a connection you can find at* **163.**

66

The accountancy firm goes by the name of D Jones & Company. As you go to dial, another message pops up from the Chief Inspector. He's run out of patience, and you're needed back at the station for an update and a debrief. That doesn't sound good.

A polite-sounding receptionist answers the phone and you explain who you are, and what information you need.

'I'm very sorry, Mr Jones is in a meeting all morning,' he explains. 'I can get him to call you back this afternoon?'

When you explain it's a murder enquiry, he simply repeats the same message. 'I can try and contact him, but he's off site at a meeting.'

'Can you tell me who registered the company, and what other documentation you have on Williams Consulting?'

'Detective, with respect, I can't. I'd need an official request to be sent over.'

'But I'm in the middle of an enquiry.'

'I understand that, I really do. But it's not uncommon for people to ring our office trying to get hold of documents. I'm really sorry, but we have to go through the formal process.'

Frustrated, you get his email address and call the station to get an official request sent over for the information. Unfortunately, your call gets instantly routed through to the Chief Inspector. You head to your car, leaving DS Lambie to follow up on the bank statements.

It's time for your meeting with the boss. Head to **80** *to see how this pans out.*

Sleep. That's what you need now, you figure. Tomorrow's going to be a busy day, so you head back to your hotel to get whatever rest you can.

You awake early after a restless night's sleep. The hotel is comfortable, certainly, but you feel uneasy. You decide to skip breakfast and head straight to the station.

DS Lambie greets you as you walk in, and the pair of you go through the list of finalists. He explains that it's widely expected one of Polly Monk (Church Fields), Heidi McLeish (North Castle) or Trevor Webber (Norton Green) will win. Could any of them have been involved with the murder, you wonder?

'Peter Maddock wasn't expected to win?'

DS Lambie shrugs. 'They might give it to his village as a sympathy vote, but nobody really thought he had a chance of winning.'

'Really? I thought he was popular? That his jam used to sell well at the market?'

'It certainly used to sell well, but nobody used to eat the bloody stuff,' Lambie guffaws. 'God bless him, but jam-making was never quite the strength he thought it was.'

'Why did he sell so much of it, then?'

'Well, people felt a bit sorry for him in the end. He was a bit of a loner, not many friends. No family to speak of, always seemed to struggle to make ends meet.'

'How could he afford his house?'

'Must have inherited it or something. Don't know.'

'Did people like him?'

'Well, a few kind souls tried to support him, but he was adamant he didn't want their charity. People started buying his jam in the end, and asked others to do the same. Problem was, it encouraged him.'

'His garden's good, though?'

'It's good, certainly, but you only have to drive ten minutes in any direction to find one that's better. They didn't have the heart to leave him off the shortlist, and that's why he and Little Norton made it to the final.'

DS Lambie checks his watch.

'Is everything starting now?' you ask.

'Not quite. We've got an hour or so to kill first.'

'In which case, I might try and get a word with one of the three favourites before everything gets underway.'

'That'd make sense,' Lambie agrees. 'Not sure you'll find anything, but it's probably a better bet than sitting here. I'll go by Little Norton to see if they've found anything else out from the scene. You steal a word with one of those three.'

You have a plan. But with the clock ticking, which of the three do you want to talk to?

If you want a chat with Trevor Webber, go to **171**.

How about Polly Monk? Head to **6**.

Or Heidi McLeish? Turn to **153**.

68

The door behind you is the closest, and leads out of the lounge into the long hallway. You take a deep breath and made a bolt for it. That's the easy bit.

What's less straightforward is what happens next. There's little point going up the stairs, you figure, as that's just going to leave you stuck in the house. On the other hand, you remember how long it took Veronica Woollaston to unbolt the door the first time you came to the house. The front door might look like the easiest way out of here, but chances are it's going to take precious seconds to unlock it in the first place.

'You've not thought this through, have you, Detective?' Frank Woollaston says calmly as he walks up behind you. He's got a point. But where do you run now? He blocks the way to the front door, and with no other option you head back into the lounge. As you run in and across the room, your foot becomes entangled on an obstacle. To your horror, you realize that obstacle is Veronica's foot. Has she deliberately tripped you up?

'It's over,' she whispers. 'Please don't get him angry. He's only a problem when he's angry.'

You look puzzled, but don't get much chance to consider the point. Frank walks in and smiles at Veronica, then crouches over you. 'Please accept my apologies, Detective. I know this may be hard to believe, but this really isn't what I wanted. You've left me with no option.'

The following morning, Veronica Woollaston goes about her business as normal. She looks sad that the competition has been cancelled, of course, but she spends the morning in the garden.

Listening to the local radio, she learns that there are no fresh clues as to the murder of Peter Maddock, and that a police detective new to the area has now gone missing while investigating it.

She finishes pruning her bush and heads back inside, leaving the garden incinerator burning away. Its aroma seems a little off, and it seems more full-bodied than yesterday. But then Veronica Woollaston always did have exotic foliage...

THE END

Go to p.293 to read your performance review.

69

As you wake up in your hotel room after a disturbed sleep, you ponder your situation. There's a murderer out there, and by going it alone and asking for the competition to be cancelled you've got little choice but to press ahead and try to solve the case. Your first day hardly went to plan.

But what next? There aren't many leads left. With the competition off, the odds are that whoever the culprit was will have moved on too. Could there be anything you missed?

Nothing springs to mind. Frustrated, you get out of bed and head towards the shower, just as your phone buzzes into life with a message. 'You need to get to the hospital,' it reads. 'It's Veronica Woollaston.'

You skip the shower and head out of the hotel in double-quick time. You get further details as you drive to Causton Hospital. She disturbed an intruder in her home last night. Somehow managed to fight them off, but she's taken a few knocks.

Something feels a little odd as you digest the information. Veronica Woollaston is fierce, certainly, but she doesn't strike you as someone who could physically defend herself. Just what's happened?

You meet DS Lambie at the door of the hospital. 'It's no use,' he says. 'She's pretty much out of it. Took a blow to the head.'

'Any leads, any clues?'

'Not really. I don't buy it that she fought off whoever it was herself, but she clams up whenever I ask her.'

'Want me to try?'

'Be my guest.'

You enter the hospital and introduce yourself, and are guided towards a side room at the end of a small ward. Lying in the bed at the heart of the room is a bandaged-up Veronica, surrounded by machines emitting a chorus of beeps.

Her eyes acknowledge you as you walk in. The steel in her look lessens. After a few pleasantries, you try and find out what happened, but you have as much luck as DS Lambie. Still, you ask a few questions. An intruder, just past one in the morning. She'd just been getting herself a glass of water and disturbed them.

If this story is true, though, surely there are two possible conclusions here. Which do you want to pursue?
The assailant must have been of similar age and strength to her. How else could she have fought them off? Ask that at **113**.
There must have been someone else in the house. Who was in there with her? Put that to her on **52**.

70

Any comfort you took from the fact that this secretive meeting is near your hotel is extinguished quickly. It might have been busy at the start of the day, but it certainly isn't now.

You pull into the car park with half an hour to spare and quickly scan the area. There's precious little activity. Anybody who was staying here has likely changed their plans with the competition being cancelled. A handful of cars are scattered around the car park, and as you enter the hotel you note that the bar is being propped up by just one or two guests.

The lighting isn't great around here, you note, and that doesn't cheer you either. You check your room for any messages, put on a warm coat and make your way to the meeting point. A sparse night staff are working and the reception desk is empty, save for a note with a phone number to call in case of emergency.

The crisp gravel crackles under your shoes as you make your way out of the front of the hotel and start to follow the path towards the back of the building. Your ears are alert for any other sound, but there's nothing immediately out of the ordinary here.

As you round the corner and see the rear of the hotel, it's not immediately clear where you're supposed to go. You check your watch. Eleven o'clock. Just past. You might just have been stood up here.

You give it a few more minutes, aware of a surprising chill in the air for a summer night.

'Detective?' a distant voice says, puncturing the eerie silence.

'Yes,' you reply, trying to hide the fear in your voice.

A figure steps out of the shadows. Something seems just a little familiar about them, you instantly think, although their half-covered face means you can't be sure.

'Who are you?' you ask.

'If I could tell you that, I wouldn't have to take all these precautions.'

Fair point, but worth a try. You note that the figure in front of you seems even more on edge than you, constantly looking around.

'I'm in danger. You're in danger. This is about much more than a flower competition,' they say.

'Then what it is about?'

'Money. And deep secrets. The kind of secrets that might have got someone killed.'

'Is this a warning?'

'I guess. But not like that. Just be sure that you really want to keep digging. I can't promise you'll be safe if you do.'

'It certainly sounds like a threat. Is it you I should be scared of?'

The thought hits you hard. You're not safe here. Might this be the moment to turn and leave while you have the chance?

Now what? You need to think fast on your feet here. Do you turn and make a run for it? This doesn't look like it's going to end well. Go to **146**.

Or is this the moment to stand your ground? They asked for the meeting after all. Go to **127**.

→ 71 ←

You jump into your car and go to start the engine. Something doesn't feel right, though. The engine bristles into life as expected, but the car feels different.

You soon realize that you won't be giving pursuit any time soon. A quick check outside your vehicle confirms the fact: somebody's deflated your tyres. You look around for the uniformed officer to call for assistance. Strange, they're nowhere to be seen.

You ring the station and fill them in on what's happened. You talk loudly, just in case somebody is still lurking and thinks help won't be coming. You don't know if you needed to do that, but feel safer for doing so, especially when a police car comes roaring along the road ten minutes later.

It was a long ten minutes, but you're still intact. During that time, you stayed close to your car and out in the open, surveying the area. Deathly silence. If anyone was out there, they're either hiding themselves well or are long gone.

Either way, you climb into the passenger seat of the car and head to Norton. You arrive a little late, but as it turns out, that doesn't matter. The fun continues over at **63**.

You lead an unhappy Veronica over to your car and hold the door open for her. She'd far rather be driving herself, but reluctantly she agrees to come with you. She steps into the passenger seat, and as you head to the driver's door, you spot her sending a message from her phone.

'Something important?'

'I just need to get someone to pick me up afterwards, that's all.'

'I can give you a lift back.'

'That won't be necessary, Detective. I've got a lot to do this afternoon.'

'Is that to do with the Villages In Bloom competition?'

'Yes. Tomorrow is the big day.'

'Who will be picking you up?'

'Just a friend. Nobody you know.'

She's telling you the basics and nothing more, and is clearly not particularly keen to get into conversation with you. The sense of unease you were getting from her has doubled now. She started off your conversation back at her house by misleading you. Now she seems scared to say anything at all.

The awkward journey comes to an end without you learning

anything new. You park up next to a damaged brick wall that looks as if someone before you'd had a little trouble getting their car into the space. The pair of you head towards the main building, a little bit of frost hanging in the air. This is going to be a long day...

Head straight in to see the coroner. Go to **23**.

73

'I'm going to try and find out what's going on, sir,' you tell the Chief Inspector.

'They won't like it.'

'I don't think many of them like me already.'

He stops for a minute and thinks, then nods. 'Keep me posted. But don't push it. They do like to do things their way.'

'I'm getting that impression.'

You walk to the front. You can feel multiple gazes boring into your back as you try the doors and find them locked. You're sure you can hear muffled raised voices, but that might just be your head playing tricks on you. Still, nobody is coming to let you in. Just what's going on in there? Is it money they're shouting about?

Finally, a flustered-looking Monica Davies opens the door. 'Is this important?', she says, as you hear a door slam in the background.

'There's a lot of people out here wondering just what's going on.'

'And you think we don't know that? This whole bloody competition was a mistake.'

You sense that tensions are on the high side. 'Is there anything I can tell everybody?'

'Five minutes,' she promises. 'Give us five more minutes, and we'll be out with the shortlist.'

'Is there anything I should know about the door slamming going on back there?'

'No,' she says, and promptly shuts the door. You head back to the Chief Inspector, who's seen all this from afar.

'Don't say it, sir.'

'Told you,' he smirks.

He doesn't get too much time to gloat, as just two minutes later, the doors to the village hall swing back open. Looks like it's showtime.

Head to **145**.

While you struggle to comprehend just what you've learned, you're now certain that Veronica Woollaston is linked to the death of Peter Maddock. You also believe that the Midsomer Villages In Bloom competition itself needs investigating, and the village committee too. Somewhere at the heart of all of this, Veronica Woollaston will be facing charges.

Back at the station, you relay everything you've learned to the Chief Inspector, who looks pretty impressed with your first few days at Midsomer CID.

'I'm sorry I couldn't get to the bottom of the murders themselves, and arrest the person who did it.'

'You don't think it's Veronica?'

'No. She's got a lot to answer for and she's looking at a prison stretch, but I don't think she's the killer. Behind that veneer, I think she's just frightened.'

You've been partially successful.

The subsequent investigations will find Veronica involved in financial wrongdoing, of embezzling funds and being complicit in the fraudulent death of Frank Woollaston.

That said, the deaths of Peter Maddock and Monica Davies would remain officially unsolved. Your best guess – and the Chief Inspector's too – is that Frank Woollaston is the likely murderer of Peter, at least. Probably Monica too. You can't help but wonder if Peter knew he was in danger too – and that listing Veronica as his next of kin would lead the investigation down the path it did.

But even as Veronica was led to the station when she was discharged from hospital the following day, any attempt to track Frank Woollaston down was coming to nought. If he was in the area, he's gone now.

Don't worry, though, Detective.

In Midsomer, there's usually another crime just around the corner. And on the bright side, at least you survived to tell this particular tale. Treat yourself to some celebratory cheese. Just a small one, perhaps...

THE END

Go to p.293 to read your performance review.

As Veronica Woollaston gets out of her car, you walk over to her. 'I couldn't help notice that you seemed to be talking to someone as you were driving.'

She's not warming to you.

'Trying to,' she admits. 'I'm not very good with mobile phones and that sort of whatnot. Next to impossible to get a signal along these little lanes anyway.'

'Who were you trying to call?'

'Monica. Monica Davies.'

'And she is?'

'A friend. And my deputy on the village committee. We have a big event on, Detective, in case you hadn't noticed.'

It's hard *not* to notice. If it's not a floral display you're driving past, it's invariably a classily designed poster advertising the weekend's festivities. Still, your pause leaves Veronica nervous.

'I'm allowed to speak to my friends, aren't I, Detective?'

'Of course, Mrs Woollaston,' you respond, as you hold the door open for her. 'This way.'

Time to head into the coroner's office. Go to **23**.

'I really don't want to do this,' he says. He slides the hood off his head and you see his face. He's right: you don't know him. The face does seem familiar to you, but it's not somebody you've met today.

'Who are you?'

'You've got what you wanted, Detective.'

He's right. You step out of his way.

'I'm sorry,' he says.

The computer base unit he's carrying is quite an old one. The stickers on the outside have faded, and the cream colour it once was has long been tinted by age, wear and one or two coffee spills, by the looks of it.

None of this matters, of course. When the computer was sold to Peter Maddock, the key features would have been internet access and the ability to play a few games – but primarily it would have been a home office tool.

Murder weapon was unlikely to have been on the spec list. You realize, to your horror, that the intruder showed his face after he disconnected the computer too. Trevor Webber won't have seen it. As the big lumpy unit travels at a greater speed than intended towards your unprepared face, you resign yourself to it all being in vain.

There's an old cliché that when someone dies, the last thing they see is their life flashing before them.

In your case, that's not true. The last thing you see is the logo of a long-bankrupt computer company. The final indignity. Not just being killed by a computer, not just that the killer will get off scot free. But also, the computer itself really wasn't very good.

Typical.

THE END

Go to p.293 to read your performance review.

Two hours earlier...

There's not much time on the first day in your new job to get settled, but DS Brian Lambie nonetheless gives you a quick tour and shows you your desk. You'd made a few trips to the area beforehand, of course, but this time you walk straight past the desk officer and help yourself to a cup of something that approximates coffee from a steaming pot on the side.

You clutch your drink as the Chief Inspector comes in and gives you all a quick briefing on the Villages In Bloom competition and the busy weekend that lies ahead. 'Let's hope it all passes off without serious incident,' he concludes.

Then the phone rings. Even before it's begun, something has gone very wrong: there's been a murder in the village of Little Norton, one of the finalists in the competition. Officers quickly scramble to head to the scene. The victim? Peter James Maddock.

'Sorry to give you a job like this on the first day,' the Chief Inspector says, with some sincerity. 'But can you go and talk to his next of kin? We need them to identify the body.'

Bang goes your quiet first day. It's over to **125**, *where you need to go and meet Mrs Veronica Woollaston.*

78

You must admit you're surprised when a young man, probably in his late twenties, answers the door of the small cottage in Norton Green. 'I'm looking for Mr Trevor Webber,' you explain, as you hold up your card. 'And you've found him!' the man grins. 'What can I do for you?'

He's confident and just a little cocky, this one. 'I wondered if I could talk to you about the entry you submitted for the Villages In Bloom competition?'

That wasn't what he was expecting to hear. 'Well, yes. Although you're better off talking to my parents. I just typed it for them.'

'With a typewriter, by any chance?'

'Yes,' he says, his eyes narrowing. 'They don't have a computer, and wanted me to do it for them.'

'Do you own a typewriter too?'

'I'm afraid I don't, Detective. I use a computer. I just borrowed theirs to fill in their form. Nearly broke it, too. Do you mind telling me what this is all about?'

Well, do you? Are you going to push him on this?

Tell him that the style of his entry form matches that of the typed note Monica Davies received. Go to **24**.
Change tack. Ask him about his parents. See if there's anything in their background that might be of use. Go to **137**.

You furiously tap at your phone, trying to get through to the station. Waving it around, you realize there's no signal. The thick stone walls of the church are blocking out mobile connections.

Perfect for the vicar giving her sermon on Sunday morning. Not so useful for someone trapped and fighting for their life. Shouting does precious little, too. Who's going to hear you? And now whoever else is in the building knows you're here.

As you hear noises coming your way, you're faced with two choices. But which is it to be?

Hide in the church by going to **213**.
Try and escape by running off to **173**.

80

You nervously knock on the Chief Inspector's door, knowing that this meeting has been a while coming. From his demeanour and the sharp way he instructs you to come in, you figure that this isn't going to be a fun conversation.

He instantly wants an update on the case, explaining that the Chief Super is putting pressure on him. He needs progress, and fast.

Which you can't offer. You've got small pieces of the case, you feel. But do you know who the murderer is? Are you any closer to cracking this particular case? He looks disappointed as you confess that you're not.

'I'm sorry, Detective,' he says, sounding genuine about it, in fairness to him. 'I'm afraid that we're running out of time here. I'm going to have to hand the investigation over to one of my more experienced officers,' adding: 'Thank you for your efforts. Hopefully more luck next time.'

It seems that you just never got close enough to this one, Detective. On the up side, you've lived to fight another day. But even though you don't know it yet, as the Chief Inspector moves on to assign fresh blood to the case, this is one collection of Midsomer Murders that's going to remain unsolved.

Some people leave Midsomer with fatal injuries. Some get on the wrong side of a wheel of cheese. Your finale is far less dramatic; you simply didn't get close enough to cracking the case.

THE END

Go to p.293 to read your performance review.

81

You know you need to get back to the house; you figure you can do it quickly and try to surprise them, or sneak back in. You opt for the former. Time is already of the essence here. You and DS Lambie turn and go back through the still-open front door.

'Where did they track the signal to?'

'The back garden,' you reply.

'I'll head there, you check the house.'

Already partially familiar with the layout, you quickly zip upstairs and satisfy yourself that there's been no further disturbance. As you head back down the stairs, you hear a piercing scream and a metallic thud.

Oh no.

You head for the back door and your worst fears are realized when you see two people prone on the floor.

One of them is a man you partially recognize. He's just about conscious but struggling to move. You waste no time restraining him and putting him in handcuffs.

The other man has a small barbecue on his head. A sizeable amount of blood is coming out from a wound just above his right ear. You look in horror as you see DS Lambie's face, the front of it almost folded in two where it's been hit. His breathing is at best light, but by the time the ambulance arrives, his heart and lungs have long given up the fight. No amount of attempts to resuscitate him come to fruition.

The resulting investigation will have significant ramifications for you. Entering a house without following due process, endangering a fellow officer. You resign before you're dismissed.

And as for the man you caught? Well, it turns out it was Veronica's husband, Frank Woollaston – but he's not talking. He faces charges relating to fraud and the faking of his own death. Plus murdering

DS Lambie with a barbecue.

But his lawyer is like an archer hitting the bullseye with the number of holes in the case. Nothing can make a murder rap stick.

And whilst you've solved part of a case with your only ever case as part of Midsomer CID, it ultimately cost you your job, and DS Lambie a whole more.

Not a great day at the office, Detective.

THE END

Go to p.293 to read your performance review.

82

You hurry back to Hazel O'Brien's house. As promised, she's stayed there, but still looks a little surprised to see you return so soon. 'The vase,' you explain. 'You ordered a replacement vase?'

She looks red faced. 'I did,' she confirms. 'I couldn't tell Monica. We bought each other the vases, and I broke mine last month. I didn't have the heart to tell her. I thought the safest thing to do was to quietly order another one, and ask Patricia if we could do it all quietly online.'

You pursue the line of questioning a little further, but you concede it makes sense. You're getting nowhere here, and when Hazel presents the broken vase, it confirms you've got up a bit of a blind alley. You might as well head back to Veronica's house and see if you can find any clues there.

Can Veronica help? Go to **181**.
Time to go to Bunbury, and the house there. That's **13**.

83

Against Monica's protests, you take the note. This is a serious threat, on the same day that a dead body has been discovered. It has to be dealt with properly. You examine the paper closely. The typed words offer no clue at first. But on instinct, you turn the piece of paper over. It's a small detail you spot, but it might be an important one.

Your fingers run along the paper and confirm what you suspected. There are slight indents on the back where the keys of a device have struck the paper. This note wasn't printed out on a computer; this was made using a typewriter.

How many people in a village like this are still likely to have one, you wonder?

You click back into action, radio the station and report the note, sharing your thought that it was written using a typewriter. 'You could do worse than see if any of the entry forms for the competition are typed,' comes back the suggestion. That's not a bad idea, you admit.

Furthermore, you can't help but be a little relieved when you're told that the entries were being gathered not by Veronica or Monica, but by another member of the committee: Susanna Swann.

'You'll probably find her at her café.' You make a note of the address and head to the village of Hayley Green, just over the river.

It's not too long a journey. The skies open for the briefest of showers as your car winds along the lanes. You flick your windscreen wipers on just for a minute, and swear you see a little piece of paper flying off into the trees. Or maybe your eyes are playing tricks on you. You hope Susanna Swann's café has some strong coffee.

As you pull up outside, you spot a woman just starting to pack up for the day, taking the few tables and chairs inside. You check your watch. It's a bit later than you thought. With that coffee in mind, you head into the café and introduce yourself.

You are not made to feel welcome. This feels like a theme.

'I know who you are,' the woman replies. 'You're the person who's just waded in and cancelled our competition without a second thought.'

Maybe you won't have that coffee.

'I'm very sorry. I presume you're Susanna Swann?'

'That's me,' she retorts.

'Do you mind if I sit down?' you wearily ask. 'It's been quite a long first day.'

She grunts and gestures towards one of the empty seats.

How do you want to play this, Detective?
You're a police detective. You need information fast. No time for airs and graces here. Go to **144**.
Ask for that coffee, and if you can just have a moment of her time? The polite approach is over at **103**.

84

You head to your car and accept that it's probably best to go and check out the crime scene itself. You're doing the right thing, you assure yourself. The chief will have you roasted in a caravan if you don't do things the right way.

As you arrive at Little Norton, you get your bearings quickly. It's a tiny village on the outskirts of Midsomer, and as you approach the flashing blue lights let you know you're very much in the right place.

After parking up, you head straight to the large greenhouse at the back of Peter Maddock's house, the place where he drew his last breath. His body's no longer there, but the rest of the area looks, from a distance, undisturbed.

You check your watch. Maddock was found around five hours ago now.

Straight away, as you approach the scene, you see it isn't ideal. People have clearly been through here, and a token wrapping of police tape around the perimeter can't disguise that. You show your identification card, step under the tape, and peer into the greenhouse.

It's big, that's the first thing you note.

The second? Nothing is in its place; plants are strewn all over the floor. The unmistakable aroma of damsons climbs into your nostrils. You see a work surface in the middle of the greenhouse, where, bizarrely, he was presumably packaging up his jam. A large number of shelves in the middle must have held the multiple jam jars. Now they lie on the floor.

The greenhouse itself is situated to the side of a beautiful garden, testament to Peter Maddock's love of the outdoors. He'd never get to see if his work would win Little Norton the prize in the Villages In Bloom competition, though.

You snap out of your train of thought and go looking for clues. There must be something here, you reason. You approach a uniformed officer, who introduces himself as PC Connelly. He's a little abrupt, but tells you the basics. Maddock had been working in the greenhouse, busying himself around the garden.

He lived alone, and had hung a 'Do Not Disturb' sign on his door of the greenhouse. Not that anybody was ever likely to disturb him. He wasn't known to have a large circle of friends, and nobody seemed to know much about his family.

He'd been in the greenhouse presumably because he was trying to get everything he needed to do completed in time for the competition.

He'd been hoping to sell a few additional jars of his jam to earn a few extra pounds, you learn. According to the neighbours, he used to do well at the weekly market selling his wares. Judging by the smell of fruit, he didn't skimp on the ingredients.

Apart from him being short of funds and a fine jam-maker, though, you're not learning much here. There's no sign of a robbery. Someone must have crept up behind him and smashed down two shelves of jam on top of him. At least, that seems to be the consensus here.

Want to take a closer look at the murder scene? Jump to **174**.
Might you be better off going around the rest of the garden and looking for clues there? Go to **186**.

You head back to the hotel and call the station. The duty officer scribbles down some notes and promises that support will be with you soon. In fairness, it doesn't take long to arrive, either. After 15 minutes or so, you hear tyres approach and see a flashing blue light. The car parks up, another unmarked vehicle following it.

The two vehicles stop, and in the second you see the Chief Inspector in the passenger seat. If you need any reminding of just how serious all of this is, then his presence is surely it. He exits his car and walks towards you. It would be fair to say that he doesn't look very impressed.

'Detective,' he grunts.

'Sir,' you reply.

You explain what happened. The note, the secret meeting, the turning away and heading for safety at the last minute. He mulls this for a minute and turns to the uniformed officers who accompanied him. 'Have a look around,' he says. 'I don't expect you'll find anything, but we may yet get a stroke of luck. No thanks to the Detective here.'

They scurry away to search the grounds, looking for any kind of clue. Needless to say, they don't find one.

The Chief Inspector turns his attention to you. 'Let me get this straight,' he says.

'On your first day, as part of a serious murder enquiry, you made the decision to withhold what could have been a crucial piece of information. As a consequence of that...'

'But—'

He shoots you down with a glare.

'As a consequence of that, Detective, we've lost what could have been our only lead to solve this crime.'

'But what choice did I have?' you protest.

'You had the choice to discreetly tell one of your colleagues,' he thunders. 'To work as part of a team. To work together to solve the case. Instead, you decided to go off on your own. I'm only grateful you came to no harm yourself.'

You look shellshocked. He sees that, and starts to be a little more good cop than bad cop.

'I know this has been a difficult day. I'm sorry, I'm feeling it a bit too. Let's all get some sleep once they've finished the search here, and start again in the morning.'

It's not worth arguing. Head to **69***, and see how things go in the morning.*

86

You walk away from Trevor Webber's house, trying to contain your anger. You know you can't force your way into his house and realistically, you can't even be sure he's hiding something. He might just be an unpleasant, arrogant young man. You're growing less convinced about the typewriter lead, but it would help to be certain. You decide to call through to the Chief Inspector to get permission for a search of Trevor Webber's property.

He's polite on the call, wanting to support the latest recruit to Midsomer CID. But it soon becomes clear you've got no chance here.

'I understand you wanting to follow up the lead, Detective, but I fear you're reading too much into a typed note. I've certainly not got cause to go for a warrant for Trevor Webber's house. Our case would have to be pretty bulletproof, given that he's the son of the richest people in the area.'

'The richest?'

'This area has plenty of wealthy people, Detective, but Alice and Geoff Webber are not short of a few funds, let's put it that way. They've invested in a lot of things around the area. They're not worth getting on the wrong side of.'

'What about Trevor?'

'He's just a hothead. Someone people indulge because of his bank balance and his family tree.'

'You think there's anything here at all?'

'I'm afraid I don't. If I were you, I'd knock off for the night and pick the investigation up again in the morning. It's getting late.'

He's right about that. Reluctantly, you decide to call it a day and head to your hotel for the night. *Tomorrow starts over at* **69**.

87

There's a bandage on the side of DS Lambie's head as you spot him across the waiting room at the doctors' surgery. He's sloshing around a pretty unappetizing cup of coffee in a thin paper cup. You'd worry it might burn his hand, but there's barely a whiff of steam coming off it.

He spots you and gives you a brief acknowledgement as you walk over.

'Quiet morning?' you joke, trying to break the ice.

'You could say that,' he says, his shoulders slumping.

'Want another coffee?'

'I've barely drunk this one,' he admits.

'What happened?'

'Been trying to work that out myself. I'd had a look around Maddock's house, but not really found anything. He was an enthusiastic gardener, though, I'll give him that.'

'What makes you say that?'

'It looks like he'd bought half a garden centre when I went rooting around his cupboards. He might not have been Midsomer's best gardener, but he was clearly its most enthusiastic.'

'Any weedkiller in there?'

'I'd guess so. Pretty much everything else is in there. Why do you ask?'

You tell him about the sabotage of Old Norton. 'You think Maddock did it?'

'Couldn't tell you. But this whole mystery is getting murkier. What do you remember about the attack?'

'Not much. I'd parked on the outskirts of the village so I could have a quick look around the place, talk to a few people.'

'And did you?'

'Yeah. Some interesting stuff too. Not much love for the committee over there. Apparently, Veronica herself was over there the other day. Sounds like everybody gave her a wide berth, too.'

Interesting, you think. At the start of all of this, she tried to pretend she barely knew Peter Maddock. Had she paid him a visit just a few days before?

'Any lead on who attacked you?'

'No,' he shrugs. 'Odd though. I thought I'd been followed to Maddock's house. Perhaps it's someone who didn't like me asking questions about the committee?'

He leaves a beat, still chewing this over. 'Never saw them coming. Must be getting rusty. Just... dunno, felt a hit on the side of my face'.

He's clearly frustrated, kicking himself a little.

'You going to be okay?'

'Yeah,' he says. 'The doc's told me to just rest here for a little bit, though. You okay for the rest of the morning? I'll be back a little later.'

'I'll have to be,' you grin.

You check your watch. The judges will be out and about around Midsomer now. Perfect. That means the committee should all be gathered back at Old Norton Village Hall. It might be time to have another word with them. Find them at **50***.*

'Heidi McLeish,' you say. 'Is there any reason you can think of that Peter Maddock would want her dead?'

'I was as shocked as you when I read that. But I don't think that was ever Peter's nature,' Susanna says. 'Of course, you never fully know anybody, I suppose. Peter did have a bit of a temper, but we all thought he was a bit of a softie really.'

'Why would he write that, do you think?'

'Honestly? Because he seemed absolutely certain he was going to win. He was telling everybody.'

'Just a bit of bravado, surely?'

'Perhaps. But what if it wasn't? Some people have been a bit unhappy about the competition anyway. I've had one or two messages come through accusing us of a stitch-up.'

'And is it?'

'Well, I can assure you that my part of it all isn't, Detective,' she says.

But what if it was fixed? What if Peter Maddock was given reason to believe he was going to win?

'Thank you for your time,' you say to Susanna, after a brief pause. 'I think you need to go off to the village hall. I presume the judging is nearly complete. I'll follow you in a few minutes.'

Susanna gets back into her car. 'I hope you catch whoever killed poor Peter,' she says, as she starts to drive away.

So do I, you think. So do I.

Before the competition announcement, do you want to have one last look around Peter Maddock's home? That's at **184**. *Or it's off to the village hall at* **63**.

'I don't believe we've met,' you say, trying to steady the perfectly obvious nerves in your voice.

'This is Frank,' says Veronica, sounding a little scared herself. 'My husband.'

You look at the photo on the wall ahead of you, and see that Frank Woollaston was a bulky, well-muscled man in appearance. He may not be now, but you can't assume that. You have to assume you're in deep trouble.

'The same Frank that was chewed up by a lawnmower 18 years ago?' you reply.

'Yes,' says the voice behind you, as Frank Woollaston walks into the room. Veronica takes a step back.

You have questions, and no shortage of them.

Over the course of the next few minutes, the story tumbles out of them. Well, out of him really. Veronica looks uncharacteristically uncomfortable.

Still, he details the problems their marriage had been having. Their huge financial worries after moving to the village. And then the hatching of the fateful plan with Peter Maddock. To fake Frank's death and claim the insurance. Quite a generous amount of insurance, too. A sizeable donation to the coroner, who left the village shortly after, allowed them to complete their plan. Turns out there wasn't a body at all, just an old dummy left over from one of the village theatre productions in the coffin.

Still more questions, still more answers. Frank had been sneaking into the house opposite Veronica's once or twice a year. It had been left unsold for some time, and there was always some problem or other that cropped up when a prospective buyer got interested.

It would have all worked out, had Peter Maddock not lost his job. When the local pub chain was sold, he found himself soon unemployed and short of money. He turned to Veronica, threatened to expose the whole scheme, and she paid him off for as long as she could. When she ran out of money? Well, the Villages In Bloom competition seemed like the perfect cover. Peter was certainly given the impression that he

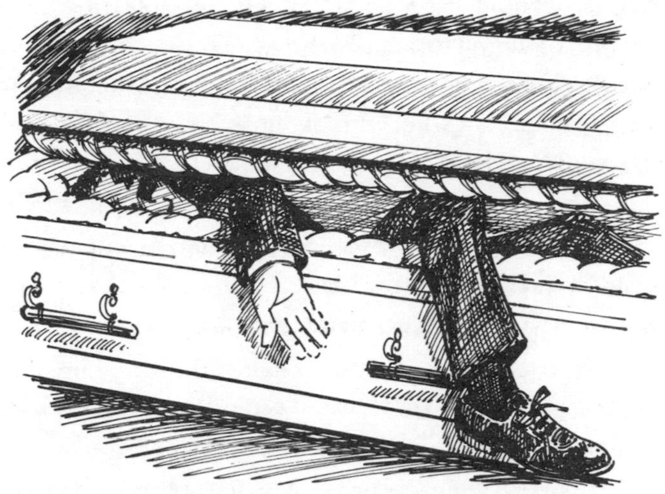

had a decent chance of winning, at the very least.

You struggle to take it all in. 'You know I'm going to have to arrest you. Arrest you both.'

'No, Detective. Arrest me. Leave Veronica. If you do that, I'll come quietly. If you don't...'

He leaves the threat dangling. If you agree to his terms, go to **26**. *If you don't, head to* **169** *to arrest them both.*

90

As you try to absorb all the news you've been hit with this morning, you decide that your most pressing priority is to get some more clues as to what's happened here.

The glass of liquid that Monica Davies presumably left her teeth in overnight is going off to be analysed, so you decide to look around the rest of her house. But there's no sign of any disturbance here. You suspected as much, but whoever broke into this house didn't, well, have to actually break in.

Your mind goes back to the vase on Hazel O'Brien's kitchen windowsill: didn't she say that Monica Davies had one that matched, where she kept Hazel's key? You head back down the stairs and into the kitchen. An upside-down brandy glass is the only item out of place, sitting on the draining board.

And there it is. A small, identical ceramic vase, with a hand-painted floral pattern on the side. Presumably this one was decorated by Patricia from the committee too. That must be Patricia Moore. You look in the vase for a key, and find nothing.

A few theories spin around your head. Maybe someone who knew about the key arrangement took both of them? Maybe they've been deliberately hidden elsewhere? Maybe there weren't any keys at all?

You dismiss the last of these. What seems clear is that someone was able to get into Monica Davies' house effortlessly, at the very least because her door was unlocked.

A thought hits you: was it unlocked? You've only got Hazel O'Brien's word for that. What if she's not telling the truth? Your chain of thought is broken as you go into Monica's living room and see a small collection of greetings cards. Clearly it was her birthday recently.

You quickly browse through them. A beautiful handwritten card from Veronica. Several from what look like committee members, at least from the names you remember. But one that stands out. A plain, non-distinctive card on the outside, but inside? A short, handwritten message: 'Happy birthday. All my love. P' with four kisses alongside.

Now what to do? Get in touch with Patricia Moore and find out about these vases? Head to **120**.
Show DS Lambie the card – could Monica Davies have had a secret relationship? Ask him by going to **65**.

91

You might not have the missing part of the jigsaw here, but there's no doubt you've just found a significant piece of it. Now you just need to get back to the village hall and try to slot it into place.

The slight flaw in your plan is that the figure in front of you has now closed the gap. He pats down his jacket and realizes whatever weapon he had is now lost. Still, the odds are very much in his favour here, and he lurches forward towards you, his hands soon clasped around your neck.

'I'm sorry, Detective,' he says, and he sounds like he means it. 'I don't want to do this. I didn't want to kill Peter Maddock. But there's simply too much at stake. And I can't have my Veronica hurt again.'

You start to feel light headed as he retains the upper hand in your struggle. His strength is pushing you backwards across the turf and you can't get a foothold in the fight. It's no use, you figure. It's no use.

Sadly, you're right. It really is no use.

Your end is quite unusual, though. It's not the moment where you stumble and find that you've fallen down next to a freshly dug grave. Nor, thankfully, are you pushed into it.

No, your attacker has found something else. It's a wheelbarrow – the gravedigger's wheelbarrow. Who knew that it was possible for such a bulky garden tool to fly so elegantly towards a human head?

Well: you, for a start. Your demise might be unusual you think, your last flickering thought, but at least it's come quickly. Tomorrow, someone at Midsomer CID will begin investigating the case of the wheelbarrow murder. Sadly, Detective, it won't be you.

THE END

Go to p.293 to read your performance review.

Hazel O'Brien introduces herself, her face puffy and her eyes betraying the fact that she's on the verge of tears. She invites you in. The houses in Green Vale seem smaller compared to the lavish residences you've seen in your brief time in Midsomer, but Hazel O'Brien keeps hers pretty tidy. The pair of you sit at her kitchen table.

'I appreciate this must be difficult for you...'

'Hazel.'

'I appreciate this must be very difficult for you, Hazel. But can you take me through this morning?'

'O–of course,' she quietly sobs. 'Monica was an early riser. Her curtains were always open by 7 o'clock. She always said she liked to have a cup of coffee and a quiet hour at the start of the day. We've been neighbours for six years now, and it's only the second time they've not been opened.'

'What was the first?'

'A few years ago. She'd had a small fall.'

'Was she okay?'

'In the end. I just about saw her on the floor through her window that time. They had to break her door down to help her, and after that, we gave each other the keys to our front doors. Us two oldies living alone next door. Seemed to make sense.'

'What happened this morning?'

'When I saw her curtains closed, I just knew something was wrong.'

'And you used your key to check?'

'Well, that's the thing, Detective. The door was unlocked, and that's not like Monica at all. We never double bolt our doors in case the other needs to get in, but we do lock them.'

'And hers wasn't locked? Do you still have your key?'

She stands up and heads to a small vase on the windowsill of her kitchen. As soon as you hear her gasp you can guess what's happened. The key isn't there. Somebody, you theorize, has used Hazel's key to get into Monica's house. And now Monica Davies, apparently innocently, lies dead.

'Where is the key to Monica Davies' house, Ms O'Brien?' you ask, your tone turning a little less friendly.

'I–I don't know. It was there. We both keep our keys in the vase on our windowsills. We bought matching vases and got Patricia off the committee to decorate them for us in the same style.'

'Who could have taken your key?'

She looks absolutely flummoxed. 'I don't know. I really don't know.'

'Has anyone broken into your house?'

'No.' She pauses. 'Not that I know of.'

'When did you last see the key?'

'I don't know. Months ago? It's one of those things that you only check when you need it. Last time was when the door swung shut and locked Monica out just before Christmas.'

You curse under your breath. Then there's a knock on the door.

Answer it at **202.**
Or question Hazel more by going to **170.**

93

You slip inside the house, cautious until you're sure that Veronica isn't still here. No sign of her, you tell yourself as you edge back towards the living room where you spoke with her earlier. You're not the least bit surprised that it remains pristine, the faint smell of pot pourri – not the cheap stuff in your hotel room – dancing in the air.

There's nothing to see here, you think. You're satisfied that everything appears to be in perfect order, and as you saw it before. There are a few creaks around the house, but you reason it's an old building. It's seen a few things in its time. The breeze outside knows just what nooks and crannies to explore so that it can maximize its unsettling background soundscape.

A dead end, you conclude. Wrongly.

For you're about to head back into the kitchen when suddenly you see it. Just by the teapot, tucked under a cup. A slip of paper. Was it there before?

You edge towards it carefully, and slide it out. In black ink, just six words are scrawled: 'I need to see you now.'

What on earth does that mean? You don't recognize the writing, but then you have precious little chance of doing so. Not on your first afternoon.

You stop to ponder as a booming male voice behind you firmly asks: 'Do you mind telling me just what you think you're doing?'

Uh-oh. You're going to need to move fast here.
You've got two options.
Defend yourself! Grab the teapot and go on the attack!
Head to **128.**
Caution first: turn around and see who it is. Go to **192.**

94

The two of you stare at each other as you both work out what to do next. You decide to take what you have.

'You'll need to come with me to the station now, Mr Woollaston.'

His face reddens as he tries to fight back tears. 'Yes, yes. Of course.'

You lead him to your car, find a pair of handcuffs and put them on him. He takes his place on the back seat as you make the journey to the station. The shock on the face of DC Isabel Carter at the front desk is clear the second she spots him.

'I–is that...?'

'Please can you book Mr Frank Woollaston in? I'm going to get a coffee. This is going to be a long interview.'

In his extensive statement, he skirts around a few details and you sense he's holding as much back as he can. But he's as good as his word. He confesses to everything: to faking his death, to killing Peter Maddock. You can't help wondering if Peter knew choosing Veronica as his next of kin would be a little insurance policy on his part. It worked, at least. It started the investigation, and got you to here.

You're not entirely convinced you've resolved everything, and you can't help but feel there's something still not quite right. Not that anyone around you is worried.

Veronica Woollaston makes all the right noises and pretends to be shocked. There's no way she couldn't have known, you think, but also Frank's statement is such that the story recorded suggests she was oblivious to everything.

Still, you're very much flavour of the month at the station. A crime solved and a deep village secret uncovered. A few days later, with the Villages In Bloom competition – which had to be abandoned in the end – a forlorn memory, there's a real sense that a murderer is off the streets, and a new asset to Midsomer CID has been found.

Until the call comes in.

A breathless police officer, who's clearly seen something awful. You hear their report, and your heart slows.

'It's Veronica Woollaston,' their voice trembles. 'I think she's been murdered…'

THE END

Go to p.293 to read your performance review.

95

There's an unease in the air here, and both of you sense it.

'Clearly you were familiar with Mr Maddock, and clearly you've not been entirely honest with me about that. But how about you tell me the truth from the start this time: why would he have listed you as his next of kin?'

'I'm as surprised as you, Detective.'

'I've only been in Midsomer for a day, Mrs Woollaston. You've been here…'

'Twenty-eight years.'

'You've been here twenty-eight years. I'm the one who's supposed to be surprised.'

'But I really am, Detective,' she insists. 'I never had a lot to do with Peter, and like most people, I didn't particularly enjoy those times I did meet him. Most of us always found him a pain… easier to avoid than engage with, if you know what I mean.'

You do, but you're not letting her off the hook that easily.

'Why would he list you as his next of kin?'

'I really don't know. Really.'

Something's obviously not quite right here. 'I don't know what I'm missing, Mrs Woollaston, but I do need you do come and identify the body for me.'

'Why me?'

You're losing your patience already. 'Because you're his next of kin, whether you want to be or not. And because he has no listed family in the area.'

She sees she's not going to win this one, and slowly gets up, heading across to her hallway to get her neatly hung-up coat.

'I'll take my car if that's okay with you, Detective. We've still got a lot to do before the flower competition tomorrow.'

Do you let her, or are you going to drive her?
Let her drive herself – what harm can that do? Go to **149**.
No: she's coming with you. Go to **72**.

96

'I'm going to secure the house,' DS Lambie says. You get up and head outside. There's nothing particularly obvious outside the property, so you walk back down the long drive. It's a secluded area, with just one or two other houses you can see.

You approach the first, and it's already clear this one is empty. A For Sale sign is discreetly position as its driveway meets the road. It looks like nobody has been in here for a while. You move on to the second, which is some way up the road. A small lane you pass seems to lead nowhere. Instead, you head up to the front door of the second house and knock. A man answers.

You introduce yourself, holding out your identification card. 'Charlie Dennis,' he says. 'How can I help you?'

'Hello, Mr Dennis. I'm just seeing if anyone in the neighbourhood has noticed anything suspicious of late.' You realize you're a bit out on a limb here, and you decide not to drop Veronica's name in. No point stirring things unless you have something more concrete to go on.

'Not much happens around here I'm afraid, Detective,' he says. 'You're better off talking to her over there,' gesturing at Veronica's house in the distance.

'Why?'

'Well, she's the font of all knowledge around here. Nobody's got their beak in more peoples' business than her.'

'Not a fan?' you ask, picking up on his biting tone.

'You could say that. If you ask me, that woman's on a power trip. But that's just my opinion, and I think I'd rather keep that to myself. What makes you knock the door anyway?'

'A murder. Two villages up. We're doing routine house calls just on the off chance.'

His face drops. 'I'm so sorry, Detective,' he says. 'I wouldn't have been so disrespectful. I'm afraid I've not seen anything. I'm a bit of an outsider really these days. I'll let you know if I hear anything.'

You chat for a few more minutes and thank him. Doesn't seem to be too much else here, so where next?

Back to HQ? See if you can pull some files on Veronica there and find out more about her. That's at **200.**

Or go over to the village hall: you've been waiting long enough. You'll find it at **35.**

97

You creep out of the house to the broken gateway in the fence. Take a deep breath. Then you step through the gate and, with your most authoritative and absolutely not scared voice, break the eerie silence: 'Stop! Police.'

The shadowy figure was just closing the boot to the car and raises their hands. You continue.

'Step away from the car with your hands up.'

They raise their hands.

'Now move your hands together behind your back,' you say as you reach for some handcuffs. You nervously edge forward as they comply with your request. This is all too easy, you fear.

As you move towards them, handcuffs ready, they make their move. They turn quickly, their right arm aiming a blow towards the left side of your head. Alert to the danger, you're ducking even as they swing their fist. Your foot moves next, aiming as hard a kick as you can muster that lands just south of their belt.

The loud howl suggests to you that your opponent here is male.

Wincing with pain, he regains his posture, and you realize that he's older than you were expecting. In shape, certainly, but fast reactions? Absolutely not. He clenches his fist, ready for another attack, then suddenly sinks to his knees. That noise is no longer a man in pain. It's a man quietly weeping.

This time, when you place your handcuffs on his wrists, he doesn't resist. 'I never meant it to get this far,' he splutters, as you lead him towards your car. He's quiet for the journey, though, so you call ahead to get someone to find out what he'd put in the boot of the car. Turns out it was evidence to try and frame someone else. His plan did not succeed.

It's still the early hours, and there's only one officer on duty at the station. They gasp when you walk in. 'That's Frank Woollaston,' they exclaim.

The same Frank Woollaston who was supposed to have died nearly 20 years ago.

Only, as you swiftly deduce, he didn't die at all. His death was faked, with the help of a retiring coroner not averse to taking a few quid. He's mum about the details, and he's keen to protect Veronica. He gives you enough to incriminate himself, but nobody else.

You suspect that the attack on Veronica was staged, as part of some kind of cover, but you lack the evidence to pursue that. The most important thing, at least as far as the Chief Inspector is concerned, is that he confesses quickly to the murder of Peter Maddock. He doesn't go into great detail, but he gives you enough. He explains that Peter was threatening and blackmailing Veronica. He felt he had to do something to protect her. And then he had to cover his tracks when Monica began to suspect what had happened.

Unsurprisingly, the Chief Inspector is rather pleased with your work.

You've managed to solve most of the case, catch a murderer and uncover a mystery that's been buried in the background of Midsomer for nearly 20 years. That, Detective, is not a bad first few days of work here.

Now make sure you're not late tomorrow. Don't want to upset the Chief Inspector...

THE END

Go to p.293 to read your performance review.

98

You bide your time. If the person inside hasn't heard you knocking, given how loudly you tapped the door, then hammering the thing down is hardly going to help.

It takes a minute or two, but eventually you hear footsteps approaching. As they get closer, it gives you a little time to admire the impressive young yucca tree growing in a pot on the doorstep. Then you hear noises, bolts being unfastened, and then the door creaking open.

A woman, in her late sixties you'd guess, possibly early seventies. She looks slightly nervous when she sees you.

'Veronica Woollaston?' you ask.

'Yes. That's me. Is everything okay?'

'I'm afraid not, Ms Woollaston.'

'Mrs Woollaston,' she says tersely.

'My apologies, Mrs Woollaston. I'm very sorry to tell you that something terrible has happened.'

You hold up your warrant card, but she doesn't give it much of a glance. Curious, you think.

But you also notice that Veronica Woollaston's face has gone a little red. You think you can see a small tear starting to form in the wrinkle of her eye.

'We've discovered a body in the village of Little Norton,' you explain. 'Do you know a Mr Peter James Maddock?'

She looks puzzled, her fingers sinking to the buttons of her self-made cardigan. She pulls at a loose piece of wool, a little irritated by it. What was she expecting you to say?

'I don't know Little Norton very well. And I'm afraid I'm not familiar with that name... I'm not sure I can help you.'

Hmmm. That's strange.

Thank Veronica for her time, and go on your way. It sounds like an amateur error, though. Go to **20**.

Politely request that she invites you in (assuring her you'll take your shoes off). Go to **129**.

99

You call the judging committee together, but, sensing how hostile the crowd is outside, they've decided to go for collective responsibility here. In particular, the chair of the judges, Hazel O'Brien, is facing this one out.

You quickly learn that she's friends with Monica Davies – the pair are neighbours – and that she's well liked around the area. And that she's a safe pair of hands for a job like this. Your questions are pointed, her deflections are precise. You push the idea that the result has been pre-ordained, and point out the unhappiness of the crowd. She, backed by her fellow judges, insists there's been no fix. You're not sold. There's too much money involved here, and every one of them appears to be wearing an expensive new cardigan.

'If you have no more questions, Detective, can we wrap this whole competition up now, please? I think this has been a very long weekend for everyone, don't you?'

That's something you can agree on. And with no firm evidence of the corruption that's suspected here, there's nothing really you can do but let the result stand. Head to **142**.

100

You waste little time getting to the point. Veronica looks thoroughly fed up of you.

'I've come into the possession of some financial statements, I'm afraid,' you say. She looks worried, and rightly so. 'Can I ask you about the finances of the committee?'

'Well, finance was always Monica's department, but...'

You leave her unfinished sentence hanging there for a few seconds.

'There's an entry that keeps coming up in the committee's bank statements. Williams Consulting. What do you know about that, please?'

She's clearly not sure how to play this. You double down. 'Mrs Woollaston, I'm learning more and more of the secrets about the committee, about the Villages In Bloom competition, about people in the area. I've learned a whole lot more even today. I'd rather you told me this, than me having to find it another way.'

She looks at you, perhaps realizing you haven't yet got enough evidence, or else you wouldn't be here. Is it worth her protecting her last few secrets?

'Mrs Woollaston, you've been attacked. You're in a hospital bed. You're in danger.'

Her mood changes.

'I know that, Detective. I'm the one wired up to this machine. I'm the one having to take medication to stop the unbearable pain. And from what I can tell, you're the one no closer to finding out who did this to me.'

'Williams Consulting?'

'I have no bloody idea,' she snaps. 'I don't know why all that money was being spent. I don't. I wasn't in charge of the money, and I can't ask Monica.'

'I kn...'

'And don't you start dragging Monica Davies through the muck, Detective. That woman was one of the best human beings I have ever known. She worked so hard, helped so many people.' She presses the button at the side of her bed and a nurse comes in.

It only takes a few seconds before the nurse enters the room.

'Please can I have some more painkillers?' Veronica asks. 'I think I need another sleep.'

The nurse looks at you, and you take the hint. Your time here is up, and you know you need to get back to the Chief Inspector. Veronica's clearly not going to talk to you, and you just hope he has a few ideas for the investigation. *Go to* **80**.

101

You move quickly to the road, and call up to Veronica's house. There's an officer outside, and you beckon them your way. Then you head back, and the mysterious figure in the house has clearly clocked you. They're hastily plotting their escape. You have no choice but to make a beeline for it, and try to stop them exiting. The front door, you figure. You run to it as quickly as possible.

What happens next is on the farcical side, but in hindsight few would argue it doesn't get the job done.

As you belt it around to the front of the house and close in on the door, you see it just start to open. Your lungs give you one last burst of pace, which unfortunately you use to trip up over the doorstep, flying at speed towards the opening door.

It could have ended in disaster, had the man inside not opened it in time and offered your head a useful cushion. You fly into his midriff, knocking him straight to the floor. Dazed but seizing the advantage, you immobilize him as best you can, earning valuable seconds for another officer to come racing around the corner to your aid.

'Bloody hell. He's dead.'

'He's not,' you reply, panicking as you check his pulse.

'No, no. You're missing the point. He's dead. That's Frank Woollaston. He died nearly 20 years ago.'

With shock, you look at his face and remember the wedding picture on Veronica Woollaston's wall.

They're right. It's him. And he doesn't look very dead at all.

It all comes out in questioning over the next few days. Even those who thought they'd seen it all before in Midsomer are taken aback.

It turns out that Frank's death was faked, to bail the Woollastons out of their financial problems. The whole story emerges. How Peter Maddock – who was a key member of the local drama group with Frank, with particular responsibility for costume and gruesome make-up – was recruited to help, along with a retiring coroner in need of a top up for their pension pot. And until Peter started blackmailing Veronica for money to keep quiet, that was that. Frank would pop into the area very occasionally and hide in the house opposite Veronica's. He's got away with that for years.

But not any more.

Frank Woollaston looks defeated as the evidence amasses. It doesn't take him long to confess to killing Peter Maddock and trying to cover his tracks by poisoning Monica Davies. The confession perhaps comes a little too easily, but nobody seems to be complaining.

As you charge Frank Woollaston with the murders of Peter Maddock and Monica Davies, and the Chief Inspector considers what charges to level against Veronica too, you're the toast of Midsomer for a day or two. Not a bad result for your first few days on the job, Detective.

Let's just hope it's a while before another murder case comes along. After all, in the peaceful county of Midsomer what could possibly go wrong?

THE END

Go to p.293 to read your performance review.

102

You drive for a short while and curse the fact that your phone has all but run out of charge. If you race back to the hotel, you reason, you've got at least half an hour before this mystery person wants to meet you.

It's a much quieter hotel you return to than the one you left this morning. Most of the guests seem to have figured that if the weekend's competition is cancelled and the area's going to be locked down in a murder enquiry, they're better off at home. Just a few are left dotted around the bar as you walk past the empty reception desk and ascend the stairs towards your room.

You work fast once you get there. You plug your phone into charge and flick it back into life. A quick call back to the station, asking for backup. You're assured that you won't be alone. No messages are waiting for you in your room you note as you slip on a warm coat and head back outside.

A car creeps onto the car park as you start to walk around the building. It's such a secluded spot that whoever wants to meet you is likely to know there's someone else driving in too. Hopefully, they'll think it's just a guest.

You catch the eye of the driver, recognizing DC Pamela Turner, and briskly walk to where you think the meeting spot is. You check your watch: 11 o'clock. All is too quiet. It's hard not to feel secluded and vulnerable here, but as the minute tick away, you realize you may have miscalculated here. 11.05. 11.10. 11.15.

They're a no show, you conclude.

And that's when you hear the yell from the front of the building.

Is it a distraction? Stay here as agreed. That's **135**.
Someone might be in trouble! Run to the front of the hotel at **61**.

→ 103 ←

Sensing the less-than-welcoming tone of Susanna Swann, you decide to take a different approach. You sit down and exhale loudly for effect.

'I hope you don't mind me asking, but would it be possible to get a cup of coffee? It's been a very difficult day.'

'I'm not in the business of giving coffee away.'

'And I'm not in the habit of not paying for it.' She gets up to make your drink. 'I really appreciate that,' you say, fully introducing yourself. 'I'm sorry to cause trouble: I'm just trying to get to the bottom of a murder, and all I seem to be doing so far is losing friends.'

A flash of sympathy darts across Susanna's face. She brings the drink over.

'It can be a tough place,' she softens. 'It was when I first arrived... I'm sorry, I wasn't trying to give you a hard time.'

'I get it. I know lots of people have been looking forward to the Villages In Bloom competition. This village looks beautiful.'

'We're very proud of it. It's been a lot of work.' She hands you a biscuit. 'How can I help you?'

'I'm trying to get to the bottom of a note. One that was typed on… well, a typewriter. I was hoping that not many people around here would have one. Might help me work out who wrote it.'

'You might not get a lot of luck with that, I'm afraid. Quite a few people around here prefer an old-fashioned typewriter to a computer. Trevor Webber of Norton Green and Polly Monk of Church Fields did their entries on a typewriter for the competition, for a start.'

'Don't suppose I could see their forms?'

'You can, but please keep them to yourself. Data protection laws, that sort of thing.'

'Anything else you can tell me?'

'Just what you probably know. Be careful around Veronica. I always find her just a little cautious and on edge. That she only tells you just what you need to know, and nothing more. I don't think her life is quite as perfect as she likes to make it out to be. I'm pretty sure she's struggling for money too, that's the rumour.'

Interesting. You drain your cup and thank Susanna for her time. May as well try and catch up with Polly or Trevor before you call it a day. Or you could call it a night and head to your hotel.

It's late. Time for some sleep. It's going to be a big day tomorrow, and it starts on page **69**.
See if you can catch Trevor. Go to **78**.
If you want a word with Polly Monk, that's **53**.

104

There's a flaw in your plan, you quickly realize as you attempt to slide out from under the bed in time to stop the intruder trying to make off with the computer. As much as you try to complete the task quickly and with as little noise as possible, and as much as the intruder is preoccupied with making a hasty exit, something was always going to go awry here.

And it does. They're on the top step of the staircase when they notice the noise you're making. As they do, your body is only halfway out from under the bed. You're still pretty much prone on the floor and, let's say charitably, not in a position of strength.

The figure turns and heads into the bedroom, catching sight of you. For a second, the pair of you look into each other's eyes, both finally realizing who the other person is. 'Y–you,' you gasp.

'I'm sorry,' they whisper, a tear in their eye. They line up a kick, and at first you sigh with relief when you realize it's not aimed at you.

It's only a minor comfort, though, when you see their actual target: the two wooden legs either side of your head. The legs keeping the heavy bed lifted off the ground. The first kick takes out the first of them. You see what they're up to. Now it won't be so obvious that you've been attacked. It'll look more as if you got yourself into a difficult-to-explain situation and an old, lumpy bed finally gave way.

Oh sure, it won't take long for someone to work out there's been foul play. But it'll take a little longer, and that's all the opportunity they'll need to get out of the area. At least, that's what you assume they'll do as the second hefty kick removes the other leg, and the frame of the bed smashes into your back, pinning you to the ground.

They don't make beds like this any more, you muse as the sheer weight of it hits, taking the wind and breath straight out of you.

Your eyes close, and you hope they'll open again. While you let that thought fade into your head, the mysterious figure jumps into a car with a computer, never to be seen in Midsomer again.

Sadly, your adventure has come to an end, Detective. The crime is unsolved.

Your own fate? Well, let's just say it's not the happiest of endings for you...

THE END

Go to p.293 to read your performance review.

105

As you process what she's been telling you about her life with Frank Woollaston, you recall the look on her face when you mentioned Peter Maddock before. You decide to repeat yourself.

'I know about Peter Maddock,' you tell her.

This time, her defences aren't quite as good. 'I don't know what you're getting at, Detective.'

'I know that Peter Maddock was Monica Davies' son.'

There's genuine shock on her face this time. This was a piece of information she really didn't know, and she's clearly struggling to wrap her head around it.

'I–I had no idea,' she splutters. 'She barely even mentioned his name. Are you quite sure, Detective?'

'I've seen a picture of his birth certificate.'

She reaches for her tea and firmly clutches the lukewarm cup, tears streaming down her face.

'H–he'd been blackmailing me,' she says through the tears. 'Peter has been blackmailing me. For years. Monica was my only real friend. The only person I could confide in.'

'Do you think she knew he was doing that?'

'I–I don't know. I don't know anything any more.'

The story tumbles out as your phone quietly vibrates in your pocket. That'll be the Chief Inspector running out of patience. But you learn that Veronica Woollaston has been running out of money, paying Peter Maddock for years. And in the last year or two, he's wanted more and more money, to the point where she's struggling with debt.

'The flower competition? Its £100,000 prize?'

'You've got to understand, Detective, I had no other choice.'

'Mrs Woollaston: why was he blackmailing you?'

She's been waiting for this question, and she realizes there's little point now in shirking it.

'Because he knew about Frank.'

He knew what about Frank? Ask that at **219.**
Does Veronica know who killed Peter Maddock? This might be your best chance to ask. Try **210.**

106

You head back to your car and put in a call to DS Lambie. He was investigating the finances of the committee and the competition: perhaps he can shed some light on things?

He picks up quickly. 'It's late,' he mumbles.

'I know. I've just left Trevor Webber's house and I'm heading to my hotel. Calling it a night.'

'Good idea. What do you need?'

‘Well, firstly, how are you?’

‘Been better,’ he admits. ‘At the end of all of this, I’ll buy you a coffee and fill you in. But right now, let’s get on with what you need to know.’

‘You said you were investigating the finances of the committee, is that right?’

‘Yeah. They’re not in a good state from what I can tell, but trying to find the exact records is proving difficult.’

‘Trevor Webber reckons his parents have paid for everything, though?’

‘Yeah, that’s right. They bankrolled the committee when it was nearly out of funds many years ago. It’s only in the last year or two that the well seems to be running dry.’

‘He doesn’t seem inclined to help them.’

‘Can you blame him? They helped themselves to his money, and then kept him on the outside of everything.’

‘I got the impression that’s just how he wants it.’

‘Maybe. I get the impression, though, that he’d just like the courtesy of knowing what his money’s been spent on.’

‘Any ideas?’

‘Nothing firm. If we can find the bank statements somewhere we might have a better idea.’

‘Can’t you get the bank to hand them over?’

‘Not enough cause, and I don’t even know what bank it is. We’ve got a very secretive committee.’

‘I’m learning that. I’m just at my hotel. Hopefully we’ll have some more luck with this tomorrow.’

He bids you goodnight as you head to your room. Tomorrow feels like it’s going to be a big day. It starts over at **69**.

107

After checking on her, you tell Veronica that you'll be back shortly, and head down to the café near the entrance of the hospital. It's a bustle of activity, but you find a seat where you can watch the front doors. Well, as best you can: your view is slightly obstructed by the entrance to the café area and the pillar hosting a menu of assorted less-than-healthy things to eat.

You nurse a lukewarm cup of coffee and try and take in everything that's happened over your first few days in Midsomer. Occasionally, an update buzzes through on your phone, but none of it brings positive news. The house in Bunbury has thrown up no new clues, and there's nothing fresh from either murder scene.

People go in and out of the hospital, but it's tricky to catch a full glimpse of their face without drawing attention to yourself. After about an hour, DS Lambie arrives and spots you. He walks over.

'Thought the Chief Inspector might send you,' you smile.

'He's tied up with the briefing and couldn't get away quickly enough. Anything?'

'Nothing I could see from here.'

'At least you're safe.'

The pair of you head back up to check on Veronica and look around her room to see if she's still alone. To your surprise, she's sitting up in bed.

'He left ten minutes ago,' she says.

'What do you mean?' you exclaim.

'Frank,' she says. 'My Frank. He's been and gone while you weren't here. He came in, told me he was going, that he wanted to see me one last time, and left.'

'Why didn't you call us?'

'How was I supposed to do that?'

Fair point. There isn't time to wonder how she knows you were expecting Frank to be here.

'Did he say where he was going?'

'No, Detective,' she says. 'He just said goodbye. Goodbye for the last time.'

You and DS Lambie head out quickly to the car park, assuming he'd come this way by car. You ask for the security footage too, but you're aware that you're looking for the proverbial needle in the haystack here – and this time you're out of luck.

The Chief Inspector calls and asks you to come in for an update. Fresh out of leads, you head back to see him. Go to **80.**

108

'Oh, come on.' She rolls her eyes as she answers. 'Just how wet behind the ears are you? The power and the money. This whole competition has sounded like a stitch-up from the start. I'd bet the house I can't sell on one of those two winning it.'

She does have a point. There's something fishy about the chair of the committee's village entry, and the son of the people funding it all making the final list. Her empty house, ironically enough, is opposite Veronica's house, but she can't seem to shift it.

'Rumours have been going around for months now about the money slipping away,' Heidi continues. 'The committee used to be rich. Veronica used to be rich. I wouldn't mind a look at their bank balances now.'

'What would you expect to find?'

'What *wouldn't* I expect to find, you mean? The word is that both of them are running out of funds, and fast. Don't ask me why. None of us can work that out. But at least we can see how they're going to top those balances up.'

'Couldn't it be that they had the best displays? If I ask them, aren't they just going to say that you're upset because your village isn't on the shortlist?'

'They'd be right about that too, Detective. And let them say it. Let them spout their holier-than-thou drivel. I'm through with the lot of them.'

With that, Heidi McLeish excuses herself and gets into her car, driving off quickly. You head back to the village hall at **199**.

109

You look at Hazel O'Brien as she continues to tell the story, yet questions are swimming around your head. Why is she suddenly telling you this now? Why didn't she tell you this earlier?

She's got no answer for that, and looks ashamed when you ask the question. 'I've been sitting here thinking the same thing. There are just so many secrets, and I just wanted it all to be okay.'

'Which it isn't. It isn't okay.'

'I know. I'm truly sorry,' she says, as she heads into the next room. She returns shortly with a couple of handwritten notes. Nothing special: 'Keep your mouth shut' and 'You're being watched.' Neither would have been difficult to fake, and even if they're the real thing, it's going to be tricky to get any evidence or leads off the back of them.

'Do you have any proof at all to back up what you said about

Frank Woollaston? Given that he's been dead for nearly 20 years?'

'He's not dead, Detective.'

'You're going to need to help me out here.' Your patience is running thin here.

'He's not dead,' she insists. 'He's not dead. He's alive. I only found out a few months ago, and that's when the notes starting coming.'

'What did you find out? And how?'

'That his death had been faked. That Peter had helped him fake it. Monica knew too.'

Who else knew? She anticipates the question.

'Veronica knew.' She's holding back tears. 'She was so scared of him. But she knew.'

'You have to understand, Mrs O'Brien, this is a bit of a story to have to swallow. Is there any proof?'

She looks sheepish. 'No. I've not seen him or got a picture, if that's what you mean. But Monica saw him. She didn't believe it at first, but she confronted Veronica in the end and...'

'And...?'

Your phone is trying to get your attention. You assume it's the station, probably the Chief Inspector trying to get hold of you. But what to do here? Hazel O'Brien has a lot of stories with precious little to back them up – and time is not on your side.

Caution Hazel and take her to the station for more questioning? That's **143.**
Or does she have more she can tell you about Williams Consulting right now? That's at **32.**

110

It's not a happy Chief Inspector on the other end of the phone. You can understand his unhappiness: two murders, a collection of possible threads, but nobody seems any closer to cracking the case.

'I'm sorry such a difficult case has landed on you in your first couple of days with us,' he says. 'Come back to the station and let's review everything,' he says.

He sounds supportive, but you can sense the frustration in his voice as well. Presumably, his superior is leaning on him to get results, and now he has to do the same to you. In his defence, at least he's trying to be friendly about it.

You've got a sinking feeling here. The Chief Inspector might have some new evidence he can't tell you over the phone. Or it might be that he's not happy with how you're doing.

What do you want to do?

Head back to the station and go to see him: you need **80**.
Is it worth asking for a bit more time? Try **182** *for that.*

111

'Without my family, Detective,' says Doreen Webber, staring at you directly, 'there would be no Midsomer committee. Or flower competition.'

It's a bold statement, you feel, but you also assume, correctly, that she's going to make a stab at backing it up.

'The Webbers have been part of this area for over 200 years. And without my family, this wouldn't be a part of the world that's the pride of the country. Look in every village and you'll see my family name. It stands for something, Detective, and – I mean no offence by this – I wouldn't necessarily expect you to understand that as a newcomer.'

'None taken.'

'When you walk around these villages, do you see hooligans hanging around street corners? Do you see people glued to their mobile phones? Do you see people slobbing around and breaking the law?'

'No offence, Mrs Webber, but I saw a dead body yesterday and it's just my first week.'

'None taken,' she says without missing a beat. 'But you've made exactly my point. This area has standards. My family have put lots of money into the area to make sure it still has standards. And just two days before this tawdry competition, it's falling apart already.'

She anticipates where your questioning is likely to go.

'My family put up the money for the competition, against our better judgement, because she asked.'

'Who asked?'

'Dear Veronica, of course. I know she's been struggling. I know the committee has been running out of money. She was adamant this was the best way forward. I wish I'd listened to my instincts.'

'Why do you think the committee is running out of money?'

'Now that's a good question,' she says, looking directly at you again. 'I wish I knew the answer. I asked Veronica, of course.'

'And?'

'She just kept fobbing me off, and always apologizes for coming back to us Webbers for more. She always thought this competition would get other people to open up their purses and wallets. Didn't work out like that, of course.'

You thank her for her time, but she catches your arm.

'Just think about this, Detective. I presume you're going over to see the judging now. Ask yourself as you watch: how can all of this have cost six figures? Why is the prize money so big?'

She has a point. But it's time for the announcements to begin over at the village hall. Best get over there by driving to **63**. *Unless you want a quick trip back to Peter Maddock's house while you can, at* **184**?

112

You hold up your identification card to the uniformed officer and quickly brief him on what's happened. He looks puzzled – you've just broken into a parked car! You're also aware that you may have some things to answer for shortly. Still, he sees the initial priority and duly runs up the path to see what the noise was.

The car alarm is still going off, and there's no obvious way to stop it. But the car itself is open now, and you reach through the broken window to unlock the door.

You sift through the empty cartons and wrappers that coat the footwell and back seat. You look around for a lever or catch to open the boot, but realize you may have to do this the old-fashioned way. You clamber onto the back seat of the car and lift the parcel shelf.

No dice, you think, as you see, well, pretty much nothing. Just a few more empty cartons, a few soft drinks and a blanket or two.

It's a different story when you pull back the compartment mat underneath the clutter, expecting to see the car's spare tyre underneath. Instead, there's just a small bag. You pull a glove out of your pocket, put it on and pick up the bag. It's got, from what you can tell, a couple of small bottles in.

You take the bag and walk back to the house. The officer runs up behind you. 'Whoever it was is long gone,' he gasps, looking at the bag in your hand. 'What's that?'

'Good question. Do you have an evidence bag?' He runs off to get one. Your strong suspicion is what you have in your hand might just be tied to the death of Monica Davies. In fact, it must just have caused it. But who can confirm that? And what was in the house?

You call the station and explain what's happened. An officer takes the evidence bag and it's rushed off for analysis. It shouldn't take long to get an initial assessment. A search of the house, meanwhile, reveals next to nothing: it's been empty for a while. Just what looks like the tag of a new backpack.

As forensics get to work on the car – that you've contaminated – at least the alarm is finally silenced.

You follow the path.

A good ten minutes has passed since the figure ran up it, and it feels futile as you attempt to trace their steps. You try anyway. You go past the broken fence and keep walking, quickening your pace.

The path winds around the empty house in a U-shape, and ends up back on the road Veronica lives on, just further up it. In fact, you can see her house from where the two roads meet, but those on her driveway are looking in the other direction.

You assume that the figure you disturbed must own the car, and was presumably in the house for some reason too. But who could it be? What were they doing? Is there something they're going to come back for? You wonder if their footsteps match those that escaped over Veronica's fence, but there's little to go on here.

Your phone buzzes as you traipse back to your car, resigned.

The trace on the abandoned vehicle brings up nothing. And then there's an update on Monica Davies's death. It's now strongly suspected that someone poisoned the solution she'd left her dentures soaking in overnight. A fast-acting agent; a woman killed by her very own false teeth.

One last possibility, you think. The chronology now seems to be that whoever the attacker was set the poison for Monica first, then headed over to Veronica's. You're guessing they set up some kind of base in the abandoned house.

Might they return? Is it worth holding out on the off-chance they'll be back? That's at **12**.
Or is it back to the station to put together the pieces you have? You need **180**.

113

As you continue your questioning, Veronica has little but a feeble defence to offer. She's not giving up much new information, but is insistent the intruder was easily spooked. She starts to get a little worked up about it, and the beeps around her get a little more intense.

'You're going to have to leave,' a nurse tells you, looking worried. She calls in a doctor, and as you leave Veronica's room, a collection of medical experts are rushing in the other direction.

Resigned, you put your theory to DS Lambie. Surely the only person Veronica could have even begun to fight was someone of similar stature to her? 'So what you're telling me,' DS Lambie replies, 'is that we're narrowing our search to Midsomer residents over the age of 60 who live in posh houses?'

He allows himself a chuckle. 'We're not going to get to chat to her again in a hurry, and that's if she fully pulls through anyway,' he says, getting more serious. 'The only person who can tell us who attacked Veronica Woollaston is Veronica Woollaston. And she's not giving us anything,' he laments.

With the murder trail now gone cold, and Veronica's assailant vanished without trace too, your first day or two really haven't worked out very well at all.

'Come on,' says DS Lambie, sensing your disappointment as you mull it all over. 'I'll buy you a coffee from the canteen. It won't be long before there's another case to solve...'

And then both of you get the same message at once. You look at your respective phone screens, then at each other.

'Forget the coffee,' he says. 'Let's get moving.'

You need to get to Monica Davies' house. That's at **117.**

114

You hadn't noticed at first, but behind where the little car is parked up there's a small path. The weather's too dry for there to be obvious footprints on the pavement, but you're curious as to where it leads.

It winds just a little, and then you realize that the path cuts in to run alongside the house that's opposite Veronica Woollaston's. You'd already clocked the For Sale board tucked just inside its driveway, and looking over the fence as the path goes parallel to it, you see no sign of life. In fact, it looks as if the house is empty. Presumably the owner has moved on? Maybe even passed away?

You don't quite see it at first glance either, but it's hard to mistake at second. A small gate built into the fencing, leading to the property. You try it: it's locked, but easily rattled. It doesn't feel like it would be too tricky to force, given that the fence itself is in a state of disrepair.

You look ahead. The path seems to wind around the house in a U-shape. Do you want to keep following it? You need **152.** *Or do you want to try and force the gate? Risky, but it's over at* **28.**

115

You cautiously approach the telephone. It's quaint to see an old-fashioned answerphone attached to it with a tape inside, but then you chuckle as you allow yourself to think that a fair few Midsomer residents might have a similar set-up.

Still, the stark LED indicator on the front tells you that Peter Maddock has two messages. If he'd been working in the garden, you reason, he'd have put the machine on. These messages are likely to have come through this morning. Late last night at an absolute push.

You take out your smartphone to record the messages as they play.

The first is Monica Davies, and she's talking about damsons. 'Peter, it's Monica,' she says. 'I've checked the space, and yes, you can have a slightly bigger table for your jam. Please don't go mad, though. We're still tight on space for the sale. See you later,' and she clicks off.

You scribble a few notes in your pad as the second message spits out of the machine.

'Peter,' says a disguised voice. 'I told you not to do this.' The caller clicks off. The machine is too old to have any kind of time stamp on the message. You're left with guesswork, and you assume that whoever it was left it at best hours before Peter was killed. And they also wanted to be heard.

Either Peter would have found the message. Or, more likely, the word would spread that he'd got on the wrong side of someone and paid the ultimate price.

The plot is thickening, you think. You stop your phone recording and glance at the time. You need to get moving. The formalities are about to get underway in Norton, and you need to be there. Find them at **63**.

116

Shirley Ambrose is a retired officer with Midsomer CID. As such, maybe she can fill you in on a few things. You certainly hope so.

When she answers the door, you understand why people don't see so much of her. It takes her a while to answer, and she's clearly struggling to walk, even with the stick that she uses. A frame is tucked just inside her front door too.

You introduce yourself and she welcomes you in. You reckon she's got to be at least seventy-five, and she wears the weariness of someone who's not had the easiest of lives. 'I'd make you a drink, Detective, but it'd probably take me ten minutes to walk there and back,' she smiles. 'Feel free to help yourself.'

You decline the offer, and give her the barest of backgrounds. Then you quickly come to the point.

'I've been finding out about the death of Frank Woollaston.'

She takes a sharp intake of breath.

'Terrible business. Friendly man was Frank. Don't know how he ended up married to her.'

There's little doubt that while Shirley Ambrose's body may be struggling, her mind absolutely isn't.

'You remember his death?'

'Of course. Must be, what, coming on for 20 years now?'

'Eighteen.'

'Poor Frank. I do miss him.'

'Friend of yours?'

'Just a pleasant man, really. I can't say I knew him very well, but he was always so kind and polite.'

'Not everyone seems to feel that way.'

'I know. But there's not much I can do about that.'

'The file on his death though. It's a bit, well, on the sparse side?'

'There wasn't an awful lot else we could put in. Nobody really wanted a picture of him after the accident, and it all seemed pretty routine. Outside of the lawnmower, at least.'

'What do you remember about the time?'

'Well, he was working on one of his shows.'

'Shows?'

'He was in charge of the amateur theatre group. Although you'd never know they were amateur by the scale of some of the productions he managed to mount. He threw his heart and soul into them. Got into the habit of hiring a few theatre professionals too.'

'Pantomimes?'

'I think he only did one of those. No, he was very serious about his theatre. Shakespeare, classic books, that sort of thing.'

'Was Veronica involved at all?'

'Not her thing at all. She sorted out the programmes for him, but otherwise left him to it.'

'It all sounds expensive, though.'

'It was always expensive where those two were concerned.'

'Did the shows make money?'

'Don't be daft. Used to cost the committee a fortune. Wasn't as bad once they started selling DVDs of them, but even so.'

'Were they any good?'

'They weren't bad, you know. There must be at least one DVD on the shelf over there, I think,' she says, pointing at her small but tidy collection of discs and books.

You're getting side-tracked. Get the conversation back onto Veronica. Go to **49**.

Is there something in this? Get the DVD and ask a few more questions about Frank. Go to **215**.

→117←

Both you and DS Lambie pull up outside Monica Davies' house. Already, there's an ambulance and several flashing blue lights outside. The little village of Green Vale is one that hadn't made it to the finals of the Villages In Bloom competition, but it still looks pretty. Sadly, there's now a darkness at the heart of it.

You and Lambie show your identification cards and head into the house. It's a beautiful cottage, quite small compared to many of the other homes in the area. It's tastefully, calmly decorated too, and there's little in its presentation that suggests the owner likes to show off. There's no pretence: it's just a nice home for someone to live in.

Monica Davies has spent her last night here, though. You ascend the stairs and turn to the right, where her small bedroom is. A modest double bed, with her lifeless body to the side of it, settled on top of the bed covers. Her dentures slightly dislodged from her mouth, you notice, but no signs of any struggle.

The forensics officer nods as you walk in, and one or two other officers are milling around.

'What do we know?'

'One of the neighbours called about half an hour ago. Said that Monica was always an early bird, but her curtains were still drawn at 9.'

You check your watch. 10.30 now. Things have moved fast this morning.

'What time did you get here?'

'9.20. No response when we knocked the door, no sign of a break in. The neighbour let us in.'

'Who's the neighbour?'

'Hazel O'Brien. They've been neighbours for five or six years now.

Both live alone. They've each got keys for each other's houses in case there's ever any problem. Good job, too.'

'Any idea how she died?'

'Looks like she passed away peacefully in her sleep,' says a uniformed officer, who arrived minutes before you.

'I'm not so sure of that,' counters the forensics officer, rolling her eyes.

'Do you have a theory?' you ask.

She looks closer. 'I'm guessing that she got up and went to the bathroom. And then by looking at her position, I wonder if she sat back down on the bed and collapsed? It's as if she woke up as normal, but then died shortly after. Her body's still a little warm: I wouldn't put time of death any earlier than 7 o'clock this morning.'

Quite a morning it's been. Veronica in hospital. Monica Davies dead. DS Lambie taps you on the shoulder. 'The neighbour is outside if you want a word.'

That seems like a good idea. Head next door by going to **92**.
Want to take a quick look at the bathroom? You need **33**.

118

'It's going to be dangerous,' you say to DS Lambie. We need to take this carefully. He agrees. You turn to Mr Thomas. 'There's a dangerous man in there. I take it you're not going to have a problem with me trying to confront him?'

It puts him in his place for the minute. You and DS Lambie opt to head around to the back gate, rather than going through the front door.

It proves wise. There's a man hiding around the corner of the house's rear. He's more interested, though, in watching you than anything else: he seems to have some kind of weapon in his left hand, but he's taking a picture on his own phone with the right.

'Quick,' you whisper to Lambie. 'Take a picture of him.' It's a prudent move. When he sees there's more than one of you, he's spooked and turns to leave. Not slowly either: he vaults the fence and runs. DS Lambie gives chase, but to no avail. He returns breathlessly ten minutes later, as you examine the upended barbecue in the garden.

'Presumably he didn't think there'd be two of us.'

'It's a good job there was,' DS Lambie replies, his lungs gradually grasping enough air to form a sentence. He holds up his phone. 'Because that was Frank Woollaston.'

He shows you the picture. It all clicks into place. The man you saw in the wedding picture on Veronica Woollaston's wall: he's alive. And he was supposed to have died 18 years ago. And that means that Veronica Woollaston is likely to be in real danger...

You need to get moving to the hospital where Veronica is. Make sure, too, that you alert the station: Frank Woollaston is alive.
Go to **11**.

119

You take a deep breath, struggling to believe that you've been put in this situation. Why are you the only one who sees the gravity of what's happened here? A man has died, and these people want to carry on as if nothing has happened.

'I'm very sorry,' you say, not entirely believing your own words as you utter them, 'but there's no possible way a competition can still take place. A man has died in very suspicious circumstances, and it's clearly tied in some way to the Villages In Bloom competition. I'm very sorry' – *stop saying sorry*, you say to yourself – 'but I have to request that the whole thing is cancelled.'

Some people take bad news in their stride; the people in the village hall are not among them.

Uproar ensues as competing voices protest. Veronica Woollaston is the only one who's silent, but then she doesn't really need to speak. The glare she's giving you could test the resolve of the sturdiest concrete block, let alone a detective starting a new job. You elect to turn away and reach for your phone.

Your conversation is a brief one, and it's clear that your superior back at HQ isn't keen on your recommendation either. They promise to pass on your request to cancel everything, conceding that you may well have a point.

As you come off the phone, you notice both Veronica Woollaston and Monica Davies individually trying to attract your attention. Interesting. You thought those two were thick as thieves – why are they acting separately now?

Here's the question for you, though: which of the two of them do you want to talk to? Or do you just bring them together and get the chat over with in one go?

Talk to Veronica? Head to **206**.
Have a chat with Monica? Go to **2**.
Or why not save time and do them both together? Jump to **27**.

120

After bringing DS Lambie up to date, you both head off in different directions. He's going to head around Green Vale, just to see if anybody spotted anything. The villagers all clearly know something's gone on here anyway, by the cars and blue lights outside Monica's house. News does not travel slowly around here.

In the meantime, you're going to see Patricia Moore, who lives at the edge of Green Vale. All you know of her is that she's on the village committee, but still, she seems unsurprised to get a knock on her door.

'Do come in,' she says, as she answers promptly. 'I saw one or two people going door to door, so I boiled the kettle.' You make a mental note: Patricia Moore is a curtain-twitcher.

You decline her offer of a hot drink, but accept her invitation to come inside. Her house is a busy one, and in her living room she introduces you to her husband, Jimmy. Around the room, plenty of ceramics are on display, and you acknowledge them.

'It's my little business,' Patricia Moore explains. 'I've always loved crafts and decorating things.'

'How's business been?'

'Better since Jimmy set up a little website for me. I get two or three orders a week, and that supplements our pension well enough. We can't grumble.'

'Where do you do your work?'

'I've got a little workshop at the bottom of the garden. Would you like to see?'

'I'd love to.'

The garden is quite a long one, and the winding path leads to a construction that might look like a glorified shed from the outside, but it's anything but on the inside. You'd not call it tidy, but it's bigger than you were expecting, and the walls are lined with materials, pots waiting to be painted, and an area with packing materials.

You pull out your phone. 'Do you remember this vase?' you ask. 'I think it's one of yours.'

'It's definitely one of mine. Wasn't my idea, that design, though,' she says with a hint of pride in her voice. 'I only ever did a few of those.'

'Who for?'

'One each for Monica and Hazel O'Brien. She lives next door to Monica. Have you met her yet?'

You nod. 'You said it wasn't your design, though. Is that normal? Do you usually use designs that other people ask you to do?'

'I don't, not really. I prefer to do my own work.'

'Why the exception this time?'

'Monica just loved it. I think she had a partner or friend at the time who had done it for her, although she was always coy about things like that.'

'A partner?'

'Someone, certainly.' She breaks down in tears. 'Oh, poor Monica. She was always such a private person.'

'Tell me what you know about a partner?'

'It might just be village tittle tattle, but a good few years ago now there was someone who went round to her house at night most weekends. We never saw who it was. We used to tease her about it, but she always said just blushed and changed the subject.'

'Could have just been a friend?'

'It could. And it could just have been village gossips. You know what these places are like. But she just seemed happier for a year or so, you know? I always wondered if she'd found herself an arty chap. One day she gave me a couple of designs and asked me if I'd make the vases for her. I couldn't never say no to her. Such a kind person.'

Interesting. You thank Patricia Moore for her help. Now you seem to have a couple of options.

Could there be a clue to Monica's visitor in her house somewhere? Is it worth another look? Drive over to Monica's at **65** *to try that.*

Could you possibly see Patricia Moore's list of internet orders? Maybe there's something in there? Worth a try over at **134**.

121

'You said "as usual." What did you mean by that?'

'I meant that over the past few years, that committee has been run by one woman and a bunch of cronies who do anything she asks.'

You ask her to explain.

'She was so much different at the start. When she became chair for the first time, she was charm personified. But then as she kept getting re-elected...'

'How often?'

'Every two years. As she kept getting re-elected, she saw the committee more and more as hers. And she started to change.'

'Change how?'

'Turned into a mini-dictator, that's how. Started ruling the place with an iron fist, and woe betide anyone that disagreed with her. We all felt for her at first, of course. Nobody should have to go through what she did with her Frank. But look what we're left with now. A committee of head-nodders, blinded by loyalty to a woman who's spending all their money.'

'Tell me more about the money.'

'The bit we're allowed to know is the minutes of the meeting. Even those are on the short side. The committee launched this whole competition to try and raise funds. Then, mysteriously, in come the Webbers with the funding. And the rate Veronica Woollaston goes through money, you can bet some of that ends up in her purse.'

'She'll need a pretty big purse.'

'That she will, Detective. That she will. Everything seems to go through her. Everything is done how she wants it, when she wants it. And you mark my words: this wretched competition will go the same way. It's a front, I tell you. A front to make someone in Midsomer a lot richer.'

As you try and wrap your head around everything you've been told, Heidi McLeish gets into her car. 'I need to calm down.' She hands over her contact details if you need her again, and roars away.

You, meanwhile, need to make your way over to the commotion by the village hall. That's at **199**.

122

Your body tenses up as you hear a voice. You try to catch a glimpse out of the small window in the office room, but you can't see anything. Instead, you're alerted to the noise of footsteps downstairs. Whoever it is, they're now definitely in the house. You reach for your phone and send a message, asking for urgent help. Hopefully someone will get that in time. For the moment, though, you feel pretty helpless. You're aware that every movement you make results in a slight creak of the aged floorboards. There's nothing, glancing around the room, that seems immediately helpful.

You could sneak across to the other room upstairs and hide there, though? That's an option, isn't it? Although you'll need to move quickly. If you want to try that, turn to **36**.
Hang on, what about hiding out here? Perhaps see if you can get the message out via the computer somehow? That's at **155**.

123

Sometimes, you reason, when you don't hold the cards, you just have to step aside. You shuffle to the side as the bulky figure squeezes past and grabs the computer's base unit. He doesn't go through the intricacies of unplugging anything as he yanks it away, leaving wires trailing.

'The hood?'

'Not a chance.'

'We had a deal.'

'*You* had a deal.'

You stand your ground. You need to get something from this.

'The hood.'

'If I show you my face, Detective, I can't let you leave.'

'Is that what you said to Peter Maddock?'

'Nice try, Detective.'

'The hood.'

'Your choice. If I show you my face, it'll be the last thing you see.'

Insist he shows you. Go to **76**.
Give this one up, and let him escape. Go to **189**.

124

'Who's calling?' DS Lambie asks.

You pause. 'Nothing that can't wait. We need to sort through these.'

Not that there's too much to sort through, but it all seems to confirm what you've not had a chance to tell DS Lambie yet: Monica Davies and Peter Maddock were related.

'You're kidding.'

You show him the pair of faded Mother's Day cards, and the mix of birthday and Christmas greetings too. It takes a lot to shock DS Lambie, but this seems to have done it. 'I've known them both for years. I can barely ever remember them talking to each other.'

'They've done more than talk to each other. It looks like they've got a house just back there where they can meet up.'

'I don't get it, though. Why would they need that? Why would they have to keep this secret?'

Two lines of enquiry spring to mind. Number one: who is Peter Maddock's father? Number two: who actually owns the house?

Your phone buzzes again. The Chief Inspector. He'll be running out of patience with the enquiry, and demanding an update.

Which lead do you want to follow up first? Run a search for who owns the house? That's **40**.
No: do a search for Peter Maddock's birth certificate to see who's listed as his father. Go to **150**.

125

It seems it's only taken until the afternoon before you have a difficult job to face.

You drive towards the impressive house in the village of Old Norton, thinking just how perfect a place Midsomer seems to be. The picturesque villages, the winding country roads, the above-average number of drinking establishments on village greens. The surroundings suggest peace and tranquillity, and you're looking forward to exploring them.

As you drive along the lane, you chuckle as you remember the interview. It was a little odd, perhaps, that the interview panel jokily checked whether your surname was Barnaby. That moment, too, when they went strangely quiet. You'd only asked them if the local cheese was as lethally good as rumoured.

A sudden thought: have you got your phone? You quickly check, and affirm you have. Phew. It's been such a rush finding somewhere to stay for your first few weeks, until you're settled. *Midsomer Life* magazine was useful, of course, and the staff of the Morecroft Hotel couldn't have been more helpful. They almost looked relieved to have a guest.

But right now there's a death, and a slightly unusual one at that, which demands your attention. You'll have to head to the coroner to get more details a little later. But for now, you've got some bad news to break.

As you turn into Veronica Woollaston's long driveway, you recall the Chief Inspector's warning that she is the stalwart of the village. A village whose floral displays are quite something, right down to an intricate windmill arrangement on the main road.

Veronica is also chairwoman of the village committee. Quite the queen bee and the last person you want to get on the wrong side of.

You knock on the door. A minute later, nobody's answered.
Do you wait patiently? Head to **98.**
Or knock again? You haven't got time to wait around.
Go to **154.**

126

'I don't wish to be rude, Mrs Woollaston, but why have you just lied to me? Why have you said you didn't know Peter Maddock when you did?'

'I–I don't know,' she says, genuine-sounding shock in her voice. 'You'd just told me he'd died… I guess I was shocked.'

'That doesn't really answer my question.'

She pauses. 'No, I don't suppose it does. Like many, I've just always found Peter very hard work. I keep clear of him. Even Monica… sorry, I mean Monica Davies, my friend… she goes quiet when his name comes up, and she's friendly with everyone. He's one of those people who can just latch on to you a bit.'

You're not entirely convinced, but it's all you're going to get. 'Well, that doesn't get around the fact that he's listed you as his next of kin. And given that Mr Maddock doesn't have any family listed in the area, I need you to come with me to identify the body.'

'Of course,' she says, regaining her composure a little. 'I'll get my car keys.'

Are you going to let her drive herself, and the pair of you go in separate cars? Go to **149.**
Or do you insist on driving her yourself? Go to **72.**

127

It goes without saying that you're feeling the fear. Exposed, alone, with a mysterious figure heading towards you. Someone who knows a lot about what's been going on. Is this the end for you? Is this the murderer?

'I need your help,' says the soft, muffled voice. It's hard to place it. You're guessing it's a female voice, but you're not entirely sure.

Still, help? If they're after something from you, then you might just be safe for the minute.

'Why so cloak and dagger? Why are we having to meet in the dark like this? Why won't you tell me who you are?'

'I told you,' they say, patiently, 'if we met in the open and I was seen, it would cause something of a problem.'

'Will you tell me your name?'

'I can't, and don't come any closer,' they say, as you edge towards them.

You're not holding the cards here, you realize, as you look for any advantage you can utilize.

'I have to tell you that I believe Veronica Woollaston is in severe danger,' the voice says.

'Why would she be in danger?' you ask.

'Because if what I think is correct, then whoever killed Peter Maddock will now need to cover their tracks.'

'What's that got to do with her?'

'You don't see it, do you, Detective? Peter Maddock was threatening her. He wanted to make sure he won that competition.'

'Did he tell you this?'

'Let's just say I found out.'

'And confronted him with it?'

Silence.

'You killed him?'

'No.'

The line of questioning hangs in the crisp air.

'She's a loose end, Detective. And whoever killed Peter Maddock is likely to want that loose end tied off.'

The figure starts to edge away.

'Wait,' you say.

'I've already put myself in too much danger,' they say, retreating. 'Don't follow me.'

Now what? Do you try and pursue whoever this mystery person is as they slip into the foliage? Head to **9**.
Or follow their advice: get to Veronica – and fast? Go to **47**.

128

You're taking no chances. You're already on edge, and feel strongly that self-preservation needs to be your top priority. You grab the ornate teapot, the only potential weapon at hand, and spin around.

The spout crashes with some urgency into the left side of a familiar-looking man's face.

Truthfully, he's not expecting it, and he yelps piercingly with pain. His voice suddenly pitches higher, as your second swing of the pot hits him square in the eye. You've quickly got yourself at an advantage.

Or have you?

Because then it comes back to you. Exactly where it was you've seen this man before. Where you've heard that deep voice.

Just last week, as it happens, when you drove up to Midsomer for your induction, ahead of your first day.

The man, currently fully appreciating the damage that a teapot's spout can do to a human eye, introduced himself that day as DS Lambie. DS Brian Lambie. He's one of your new colleagues from Midsomer CID.

Well, he was. It's funny how things work out. It's a life lesson not often taught, but people don't tend to like being attacked with kitchenware. Brian Lambie is no exception. In the aftermath of your teapot assault, there would be two consequences.

Number one, DS Lambie – although he doesn't know it yet – will never see out of his right eye again. As an aside, he'll choose to switch to coffee from now on.

And you? Your detective days are over. Already! Sure, the enquiry will find that you didn't do it on purpose. But that doesn't stop the Chief Inspector from quietly suggesting you hand in your resignation before the reporter from *Midsomer Life* starts digging a little closer. Villagers remember.

And while yours isn't the most unusual story in the area, the

strange tale of the detective who smashed his colleague in the face with a teapot on their first day in the job will be talked about for a long time.

THE END

Go to p.293 to read your performance review.

129

Reluctantly, Veronica beckons you in.

An intricately patterned woven carpet lines the hallway and you're quick to remove your shoes. You're determined to give her no excuse to raise her ire in your direction.

There's nothing particularly distinctive about the artwork on the walls of the hall. A few watercolour village scenes and a faded wedding photograph. You guess that it's a good 20 years old, perhaps 30. It's clearly her in it, a woman with less weight on her shoulders than the one who just answered the door. The handsome, burly man alongside her is holding her hand, a firm grin underneath his buoyant moustache.

The silver frames are sparkling throughout, you notice. The owner of the house certainly doesn't skimp on household cleaning products.

Veronica invites you into her living room and offers you a seat. Her courtesies feel obligatory rather than volunteered. As she goes to sit in her armchair, you head to the one opposite.

'Not that one, dear, if you don't mind,' she bites. 'That one was my Frank's.'

You apologize and take a seat closer to hers. It doesn't feel like it's been sat in for a long time. In fact, the room around you is so perfect, it doesn't feel like anyone's been in here at all. That can't be right:

Mrs Woollaston is the chair of the Midsomer village committee. Surely she has her fair share of visitors?

'Peter James Maddock,' she says to you.

'Yes,' you say, your mind clicking back to the matter in hand. 'Does the name mean anything to you at all?'

She leaves a slightly longer pause than perhaps she should. You can't be certain. She tucks the small locket around her neck back under the safety of her expertly knitted cardigan and says that it doesn't. 'I'm sure I've seen his name on the entry forms for this weekend, but I can't say I know the man,' she says in the most matter-of-fact way she can muster.

'That's odd,' you say. You let the words hang.

'Odd?'

'Well, yes. Odd. This is, well, a little unusual. You see, Mr Maddock lists you as his next of kin.'

She's taken aback, and this time, no amount of fixing loose threads on her knitwear can hide it.

She looks at you, her head slightly bowed.

'You knew him?'

She nods shallowly.

Well, this is a good start. Ask her why she just lied. Go to **126**.
Hang on: why would he list you as his next as kin? Go to **95**.

130

'I'm so sorry to disturb you again, Mrs Woollaston. I know you need your rest. I'm just a bit stumped and could use your help trying to make sense of it all.'

She looks a little puzzled at this change in tack from you, but she's also happy to go along with it. Has the power dynamic switched in her favour?

'There's no easy way to say this, Mrs Woollaston. But... it appears that Peter Maddock was the son of Monica Davies and your husband.'

A pause. Almost as if she's working out how to deal with this herself. 'I...I... don't know what to say.'

'I'm sorry to ask this, but did you know?'

She shakes her head slowly, her gaze unchanged. 'No,' she whispers.

Did her friend betray her? What's the story here? Will you ever know?

She starts to cry. You try to ask her a few more questions, but you're getting nowhere. If feels like you've hit a dead end here, and the Chief Inspector wants you back at the station. He doesn't sound happy at all.

There's no escaping this – you need to see the boss. Go to **80.**

131

You say his name. It's the last thing he wants to hear.

'Frank Woollaston?'

'Shut up,' he screams, his hand clasping over your mouth.

You do your best to wriggle free, but he's too strong.

'Shout again and I'll kill you now,' he panics.

He's going to kill you anyway, you figure. His hands are focused on keeping your mouth muffled. It leaves you one spare hand to attempt a last-ditch plan. You reach into your pocket and feel for your phone. You're stabbing buttons in the dark while continuing to struggle. You've no idea just who or what you've dialled, but you hold the phone up triumphantly.

He looks startled.

'That's right, Frank Woollaston,' you shout, as you seize the moment to break free.

He lunges for the phone. Yet while he has bulk and heft on his side, stealth and speed are not Frank Woollaston's strengths. You're too quick this time, and he's lost a little bit of his control.

'Shall we talk?' you splutter.

He stops, the colour draining from his face.

'Hang that up.'

'Are we going to talk?'

He releases his grip and nods.

'But don't try and make a run for it.'

It's an uneasy standoff as the two of you stand several feet apart, neither really able to escape the other.

'I think you'd better explain, Mr Woollaston.'

'I'll only talk if you promise me that Veronica will be okay. That she won't get into any trouble. This is all on me.'

'You know I can't make that promise.'

'I can only tell you this, then. It was all me, Detective. Everything was me. I'm to blame, and I'll make a statement that says all of that.'

There's clearly more to this story, though. You sense that. Still, if you accept his offer, in the eyes of the boss you'll have solved two crimes in two days – one of which nobody even knew was a crime, it seems. This man is supposed to be dead, after all. How does that sound?

Take it. This is as good a result as you're going to get in the circumstances. Go to **94**.
Stand your ground. You know there's more to this. Go to **175**.

132

You sense that Polly Monk is opening up here. You're no closer to finding out if she's involved in the death of Peter Maddock, but the rivalries of the villages are becoming clearer.

'Why didn't someone stand against Veronica Woollaston for the committee if you were unhappy with her?'

'Do you honestly think people haven't tried? You really don't know how places like this work, Detective. Cliques. It's about who you know. They make it all look so open and above board, but those places on the committee are decided long before every election. Woe betide anyone who gets in the way.'

'You stood, then?'

'I only tried once.'

'What happened?'

'I was discouraged.'

'Discouraged?'

'I got invited to Mrs Woollaston's for a cup of her horrible tea. It was put to me that there were other ways I could get involved.'

'That's still not stopping you from trying?'

'You don't get it. I have a small business here. It was suggested that it'd be good for my business if I could support the existing committee.'

'And if you didn't?'

'I didn't need to ask.'

'So you did as you were told?'

'I had no choice. Even when all the money started to dwindle away, nobody would stand up to her. Anybody who even asks about it gets invited for a cup of tea, and never mentions it again.'

'Did that happen to Peter Maddock?'

'Her tea's bad, not deadly.'

'Where were you when he was killed?'

'Preparing for this sodding competition.'

'Can anyone corroborate that?'

She sighs. 'No. No they can't.'

Now what? There are a few lines of enquiry here.

Are you convinced Polly is innocent of the murder of Peter Maddock? If you think she's guilty and should be arrested, head to **44**.

Lots of people mention money. Pursue that at **204**.

133

You look at Veronica and sense somebody approaching you from behind. You count in your head: one, two, three. Then you leap up and make a bolt for the back door. You vaguely remember that she has an extensive vegetable garden in the back, and figure that whoever's behind you has blocked your way to the front door. This is your only way out.

You barrel through the kitchen and your heart jumps as you see the key in the back door. In a quick movement, you reach for the key and turn it, the door swinging open.

Two things, though.

As you pick up pace and make a break across Veronica's back garden, you realize that you're not being chased. Whoever was in the house is, well, still in the house.

Secondly, what you hadn't appreciated was the size of Veronica Woollaston's azalea bush.

You stumble as you realize you're running towards it, and turn towards the fence to try to find another way out of the garden. Bush averted, you lose your footing as the soil underneath you gives way, and you find yourself at first sliding a little, before falling. Try as you might, you can't correct your balance.

You don't have time to consider that of all the ways for a person to die, a large wooden potato planter is one of the more unusual.

When Veronica had bought it two years earlier, she hadn't been keen on the spot she'd place it in originally, just outside her back door. Now it's in pride of place against her fence, and produces tubers that are the envy of the village – but it's the last thing you see. Your fall accelerates, your head hurtles towards it. It's a coming together of two things – potato planter and human head – a union that was never meant to be. The sickening thud tells you your adventure is over.

Not just this adventure, either. All of your adventures. Potatoes, making a hash of you.

Rest in peace, Detective.

THE END

Go to p.293 to read your performance review.

134

Patricia Moore is only too glad to help. She heads back to her workshop and fires up an efficient-looking laptop in the corner of the room.

'I've had around 80 orders this year in all,' she says as she scans the information on the laptop's display. 'Would you like a printout?'

You nod, and nearly jump as a machine next to the laptop clatters into life. 'That's my old printer,' she smiles, acknowledging your surprise. 'I quite like the old models, the ones a bit more like typewriters. They don't drive you as mad with endless error messages and cries for new ink.'

She hands you the printout. There have been 81 orders in all since the start of the year – she was one out. Most of them aren't cheap, too. It's clear that Patricia Moore's work carries a price, with most of the items selling for between £100 and £200. Your eyes are drawn to some that appear to be gifts, though, ordered by people in the area and then sent elsewhere.

Of particular interest, is an order that Monica Davies made three weeks ago. Not for herself either. For someone else entirely – Phillip Smith – and sent to an address that you quickly tap into your phone's map. Somewhere half an hour away.

Who is Phillip Smith? And why is Monica Davies buying him a present?

Another order then catches your eye. Hazel O'Brien. Buying a vase for herself. Why would she order it when she could just walk across the village and ask?

Two leads there, Detective. One of them is likely to eat up a lot of time, though.
Go back to Hazel and investigate her order at **82.**
Drive over to Phillip Smith's address in Bunbury by going to **13.**

135

You're here for a reason, you figure. You can't get distracted. Whatever's happening at the front of the hotel, DC Turner will be able to handle it. Instead, you wait. Still nothing, though. No more noise from the front of the hotel. Certainly nothing happening here. At the very least, you figure that you've spooked whoever it was and they've beaten a retreat – if they were even here in the first place.

Eventually, you head back around the front of the hotel, some twenty minutes later. DC Turner tells you that she was dealing with someone slightly the worse for wear, who's gone up to bed now. She's going to call it a night.

Perhaps you should, too. But as you wave DC Turner off, you're drawn back to your car. A small note on the windscreen. 'I was trying to help. I asked you to come alone. You're on your own now.'

You curse to yourself. Then you turn the piece of paper over. Three words: 'Follow the money.'

Interesting. What could that mean?

You look at your watch, and decide to call it a night. You're going to need to be at your best tomorrow as the investigation continues over on **69.**

136

You track down PC Thomas Eliot, the officer who responded to the initial call. It turns out that Veronica dialled 999 herself. When PC Eliot got to the house, he explains, the back door was open and he found Veronica struggling for breath on her kitchen floor. She'd taken quite a whack, but he couldn't see just what she was hit with. His best guess is the Le Creuset casserole dish on the surface above her, given that it's about the only item in the kitchen – apart from the broken glass – that doesn't appear to be in its proper place.

She didn't give him much information, he reports. Just the basics: she came downstairs to get a drink, and there was someone there.

'One thing, though,' he offers. 'I don't know why she had to come downstairs for a drink. There's a bathroom next to her bedroom. Seemed a long way to go if she was just a bit thirsty.'

He's got a point. You try to trace her steps. She's come down the stairs, got to her kitchen, been met by someone who was already in the house, been attacked, got to the phone on the wall next to her cooker, and then collapsed, waiting for help.

In the meantime, a few hours later, her best friend has been killed. It certainly couldn't be Veronica – she's pretty much got the perfect alibi here. But surely the two incidents are related in some way. What's the missing piece of the puzzle you're not seeing?

'I'm not going to lie to you,' he says, 'I've seen more complicated crime scenes. No forced entry or anything. It's as if someone was able to walk in, assault Mrs Woollaston and leave without any alarm being raised.'

'Have you been on many crime scenes in Midsomer?'

'One or two,' he admits. 'Usually it takes a while to get the lie of the land. Not here. Just a bit too convenient if anything. That's one of two things that stand out. The other is those footprints out in the garden.'

'Anything on them?'

'Not really. Not expecting anything either.'

You thank him for his time and head back outside.

But now what? Do you want to follow the footsteps to see where they lead? Head to **22.**

Or you could go back and take a look at the car? That's at **198.**

137

As you see Trevor Webber become irate – and you sense that this is a man whose temper is not on the long side – you opt to follow a slightly different path.

'I'm new to the area, Mr Webber,' you explain. 'Perhaps you could tell me about your parents?'

He pauses, and his features calm slightly. He breathes out and your nostrils register that he's had more than one drink this evening.

'You really are new to the area,' he says. 'Alice and Geoff Webber. They've lived round here all their lives, and from what I can tell have never owned a piece of technology in their life.'

'Old fashioned?'

'You could say that. Dad made his money the long way around and sold out at the top.'

'What did he do?'

Trevor beckons at the building across the road. A small pub by the name of The Spanker Inn.

'He ran a pub?'

He laughs. 'Quite a lot of pubs, Detective.' You spot the brewery name and the penny drops. Webbers Inns. Of course.

'By the time he decided he'd had enough, he had 60 pubs in villages around the country. He cashed out at the right time.'

'Always villages?'

'Mum and Dad are all romantics like that. They always said that village life has made them the people they are today. That's why they've put so much into the area.'

'What do you mean?'

'Well, they paid for the Villages In Bloom competition for a start,' he says. 'Paid for the committee. Paid for the village hall. They're very into giving something back.'

'And you're not?'

'It's my inheritance, Detective,' he smiles. 'I'd rather they save some for me. Mind you, they're getting fed up with it all now.'

'I still need to get to the bottom of this note,' you say, now that you have a bit more of his confidence. 'I genuinely can't help you,' he says. 'Their typewriter broke. Dad took it to his shed to try and fix it. Sadly, DIY isn't really his strength. Go and check with them if you want.'

'Who is it?' says a female voice from inside the house.

He looks back into the house and back at you. 'If that's all, Detective?'

You figure you're done for the moment. But he's given you a couple of interesting leads here. Which do you want to follow up?

The apparently broken typewriter? You'll need to see if you can catch Geoff Webber and find out if the story's on the level. Go to **209.**

There's a lot of money swishing around here. Maybe you can try and find DS Lambie to see if he knows a bit more about it? Go to **106.**

138

You click quickly on Trevor Webber's name. As one of the younger people involved in the competition, in theory he should be relatively technology savvy. This theory is correct. You see his picture appear on the screen, although you can't hear him. The headset is still plugged in. You flick the screen off: you don't want the intruder to know they're being watched.

The creak of the stairs. Here they come. Under your breath, you hope that Trevor doesn't hang up, as a hooded figure arrives in the doorway and sees you. You gulp. Here we go.

You're taken aback at first when you realize that the person in front of you, blocking your exit, is not only wearing a hood to disguise themselves, but also appears to be wearing a police uniform. Could it be the officer from outside? No, a different build. Smart, though. They'd have been able to get into the house without causing any suspicion.

Who is this person in front of you? You scramble together a bit of confidence to try and find out.

'Aren't you going to introduce yourself?'

'You must be the detective,' a male voice responds.

'I am. And I'm wondering what you're doing creeping through the house of a man who was murdered yesterday.'

He pauses, his face still disguised.

'Please just get out of my way,' he says.

'Why?'

'I just need to get something, then go. Please don't stop me.'

'Why?'

'Detective. I mean it.'

Whatever he wants, there's little doubt he's going to try and get it.

'Take the hood off and tell me who you are, and I'll get out of your way.'

'You don't know me. It doesn't matter.'

'Then at least take the hood off.'

'Get out of the way first.' His voice is getting angrier. You sense you don't have an advantage here.

You're on your own with this one.

You can get out of his way. Head to **123.**
Or you can stand your ground. That'd be **140.**

139

As you pull into the village of Old Norton, you instantly see that pretty irreparable damage has been done to its displays. Perhaps some kind of strong weedkiller, as suspected. Only a windmill display at the entrance to the village looks untouched.

A smiling woman approaches you. 'You must be the new Detective.'

'I am,' you nod. 'And you are?'

'Elaine Deandy. I was in charge of the Old Norton flower displays. Or what's left of them.'

'I'm sorry,' you say, earnestly.

'Thank you.'

'I don't suppose you've got any idea what happened here?'

'I didn't see anything, but it looks like some kind of weedkiller. Who knows which one they used? Some formulas work faster than others. They could have done it days ago, in truth, and I wouldn't have noticed.'

'Any ideas who?'

'No, but that's the problem with having such a stupid prize for a competition like this. You offer a huge sum like £100,000 for a flower contest and that's going to turn heads. Especially with all the money rumours.'

'Money rumours?' 'Tittle tattle, really. Lots of whispers that the committee or Veronica Woollaston are short of funds. Possibly both. Who knows?'

Interesting.

'You don't sound upset about the damage to the display here?'

'I'm upset that someone was murdered, Detective. But I'm not going to lose sleep over a flower tournament. I love gardening and

I do it for pleasure. I'll just start again, prize money or not.'

Do you want to head over to the village hall now? That's at **50**.
Or you could ask Elaine about the size of that prize pot? If so, you'll be popping over to 7.

140

The two of you stare at each other.

'I just need the computer, I don't want you,' says a male voice.

'Who are you?'

'Nobody you know. Just get out of my way,' he says. You're completely in the dark here. You've got nobody on the other end of the webcam, and you don't recognize the voice at all.

The figure is dressed in a police uniform, but his shape and size don't match that of the officer outside. Is it a real police officer in front of you? You very much doubt it.

As you're trying to puzzle out what to do next, the decision is made for you. The intruder pushes you backwards and grabs the computer's base unit. Before you can pick yourself up, he's got it, leaving leads tangling behind as he races back out of the door.

You lurch and grab one of the leads left dangling from the unit itself. The long, thick power cable that's dragging behind it. The intruder exclaims loudly, his choice of language on the coarser side of the Queen's English.

He stops and turns back to you, the cable wrapping around the bannister at the top of the stairs. As you jump forward to try and stop him, he moves quicker. Before you know it, the cable is around your neck, his strong grip tightening it. You gasp for air as he drops the computer unit into your midriff. It takes the wind out of you, and the computer cable, snake-like, cuts off your intake of oxygen. You try and scream for help, but he drops the machine again. They really don't make them like they used to, you think, wishing Peter Maddock had opted for a laptop instead.

When they find you, around an hour or two later, you're dangling from the bannister, the cable of an old Windows XP computer ultimately ending your days.

On the up side, the cable is intact, and can be recycled for future use. On the down side? Unfortunately, you can't...

THE END

Go to p.293 to read your performance review.

141

Reasoning that you've got to try and get inside the car, the next challenge is to find something that'll let you do just that. There's nothing in the back of your own car that could help, and if you went back to it, that might just draw attention to you. The village is so well kept that there's not even a spare brick lying around you can aim at the car window.

Checking again to make sure that nobody's watching, you see that all the focus seems to be on Veronica's house around the corner. You try your elbow against the car window. Nothing. Fist or foot, you ponder, and opt for the latter. You raise your leg and swing your foot at the passenger window of the car. This time you're more successful.

Two things happen.

Firstly, the window gives way, the glass offering precious little resistance.

Secondly, something that tells you that you may have miscalculated. The car may be old, but that doesn't mean it doesn't have an alarm. A rather loud alarm, and it's now going off.

As it blares, you hear a clatter from the house next door. Was something or someone disturbed? Then comes the shout of an officer running around the corner. Meanwhile, the car you wanted to examine is beside you, but you have a quick decision to make.

You could run up the small path to see if you can find out who or what made the clatter? That's at **190.**

Or wait for the officer, explain, and search the car. Go to **112.**

142

In the end, nobody was happy.

Veronica Woollaston and her Old Norton village may have won the Villages In Bloom competition, but after all the drama there was no money to hand out anyway.

The Webbers, fed up with the way the village committee had operated, and the manner in which the competition had spiralled out of control, withdrew all of their funding.

Over the coming months, the committee itself would fold, and the friends it brought together would drift away. Nobody would mention the flower competition again.

The murder of Peter Maddock was never solved. The deep divisions in the community were permanently exposed, and fewer Christmas cards were around each December.

As for you? You survived your first weekend in Midsomer, and that's something to be grateful for. But sadly you didn't solve the case.

The truth is that there's a murderer out there somewhere. Perhaps hollowing out a television set. Perhaps sabotaging an exercise bike. Maybe contemplating sabotaging the controls of someone's wheelchair. But for the moment, they are entirely at large.

Sleep as easy as you can, Detective. Better luck next time...

THE END

Go to p.293 to read your performance review.

143

You've heard enough from Hazel O'Brien. There are too many questions for her to answer here, and she's simply not giving you anything you can do anything with. Hopefully, someone back at the station will have more luck. You ask her to come to the station with you, fearing you'll have to arrest her if she says no. Yet there's something genuine here: she wants to help the enquiry, but doesn't quite know how.

When you arrive, she goes off to be interviewed, but it's the same problem. She's only got a small part of the puzzle, and as the clock ticks by, you fear any chance to solve this case is ticking away with it.

As you watch the interview through the glass, you get a tap on the shoulder. The Chief Inspector is now insisting he has that word with you. Head to **80**.

144

'I understand you're not happy with me,' you say. 'You have something that I need.'

'Go on.'

'I gather you're the person in charge of the entry forms for the Villages In Bloom competition?'

'I am.'

'I need to see them, please.'

'That won't be possible.'

'Why?'

'Data protection,' she says. 'I was told I had to be entirely neutral, and keep them safe. And not to share the information. There's been enough arguments about this competition already. All for nothing, it seems.'

'I'm not asking,' you say, wearily, as you hold up your identification again.

This does not go down well, but at the very least, Susanna Swann is someone who respects rules and laws. Silently, she heads through the door behind the counter of the café, and you hear her climb some stairs. She returns a minute later with a beautifully organized file.

'I can't let you take them away. You'll have to look through them here.'

You figure this isn't a fight particularly worth having, and you leaf through the forms. A mixture of beautiful handwriting and one or two printed entries. But you might just have found something. Two of them appear to have been typed.

You read the names of the people who submitted them. Trevor Webber of Norton Green and Polly Monk of Church Fields. You jot down their addresses and thank Susanna Swann for your time. She curtly bids you farewell and you head back to the car.

You check your watch. You reckon you've got time to go and see one of these people now. Which should it be?

Trevor Webber: that's a name that feels like it should be familiar. See if you can catch up with him. Go to **78.**
Polly Monk? You've not heard that name, but you know that Church Fields was one of the favourites for the competition. Perhaps you should see her. Go to **53.**

145

The doors open and the committee members file out towards the stage that's been constructed. Most of the committee seem to be there, but it's Veronica Woollaston and Monica Davies leading the way to the platform, joined by Doreen Webber and Deirdre Foot. They all look a little fraught. It doesn't look as though the last hour or so has been a lot of fun.

It's Veronica Woollaston who steps up to the microphone, and starts talking.

'On behalf of the village committee and the Midsomer Villages In Bloom organizers, I'd like to welcome you to this announcement of the three top places in our competition. I'd also like to apologize,' she shrills, 'for keeping you waiting. Thankfully, the weather has looked after us.'

'Get on with it,' someone mumbles from the crowd, more audibly than they may have intended.

Veronica Woollaston looks a little flustered, and she reads strictly from her notes. Not a single mention of Peter Maddock is to come.

'It won't come as a surprise to any of you who have been driving around our villages over the last few weeks to declare that the standard of entries has been extraordinarily high. I'm delighted to say that the committee has decided, as well as the prize money, that the winning village will be entered in the national competition too.'

Murmurs of impatience from the crowd are growing. She continues, picking up the pace.

'Without further ado, I would like to announce the final shortlist of three villages, and their representatives. We will then come back here at six o'clock to announce the overall winner.'

Finally, the crowd quietens.

'In no particular order,' she says, 'the judges have decided that the three villages to make it to the very final round are Norton Green, represented by Trevor Webber.'

A loud groan, with a smattering of applause.

'Church Fields, represented by Polly Monk.'

More upbeat applause this time, with a foundation of some actual enthusiasm.

'And Old Norton, represented by Elaine Deandy.'

This time, there's applause. Quite loud applause. Veronica's village: they all know which side their bread is buttered.

Well, that is until the applause is interrupted.

'I knew it,' says Heidi McLeish of North Castle, as she loudly gathers her things and storms away from the stage area. 'I absolutely knew it.'

Sour grapes? Or is there something more there? The presentation party breaks up quickly as Heidi McLeish moves at speed towards the car park.

Do you follow her and find out what's what? Or do you try to catch Veronica Woollaston and find out what just happened in the village hall?

To chase Heidi McLeish, go to **187**.
To track down and confront Veronica, go to **57**.

146

This isn't worth the risk, you quickly conclude. You've got everything to lose here, and you're not sure you've really got that much to gain. You'd far rather take your chances with your existing lines of enquiry than trust whoever's in front of you here.

You turn and start walking quickly back to the safer grounds of the hotel's better-lit front. You allow yourself a quick glance behind you. Whoever it was doesn't appear to be chasing you. In fact, whoever it was seems to have disappeared altogether.

You head to the main entrance of the hotel. That's odd, you think. The door seems to be closed. Then you remember: the front door is locked at 11 o'clock. You need to ring for attention to try and get back in.

The sound of crunching gravel catches your ear. You breathe out, as you realize whoever it was is heading in the opposite direction, back across the car park.

The front door swings open behind you. 'Sorry,' says an out-of-breath receptionist. 'There are only two of us working and I was just helping in the bar.' You smile and thank them, and head inside.

But something makes you turn. Why did they walk *back* across the car park? Whoever it was could surely have slipped away without risking being seen?

Suddenly, a thought hits you. 'Keep this door open and wait for a minute,' you say, a panic rising in your voice. The startled receptionist nods, as you rush across the car park to your vehicle. You cautiously walk towards it and lift the windscreen wiper. Another small note, just like the first.

You look around. Nobody. You pick the note up and dash back to the light of the hotel. You exhale in anger as you read the words. 'I only wanted to help you,' reads the hastily scrawled writing. 'I won't be back.'

You sigh. You seem to have lost your only lead here.

Is there any way to save the situation? Urgently call for support and get the area searched. Head to **85**.
Call it a night, and hope that there are further leads you can follow in the morning. Head to **69**.

147

You look across to see how far away the button is that will alert a nurse if assistance is needed. If you had your strength, you might just about stand a chance of getting to it. The hard truth you're facing now is that you don't have that strength, and you feel yourself getting weaker by the minute.

You look to Veronica, but she seems frozen, her eyes never leaving Frank. What's going on in her head? Where do her loyalties lie here? Is she just plain scared?

Your best option, you swiftly realize, is to call out for help. You take a breath and get ready to yell.

But you can't.

The power in your lungs just isn't there. What you intended to be a cry for help barely comes out at talking volume. Frank looks at you. 'Not a good plan, Detective,' he quietly says. 'I'd save your energy. You're going to need it.'

Your head is swirling. Frank's talking to Veronica now, but you can't fully make out what he's saying. It seems to be some kind of goodbye.

She knew he was alive. She's always known he's alive. And yet there's an air of fear about her interactions with him. The two are still talking as your eyelids crash down, the sheer weight of them making resistance impossible.

Will you wake up from this? You're not sure. Your head spins with questions, fighting against the throbbing pain, as you feel yourself collapsing back into the chair you're sat on.

And then darkness.

The faint sound of a door opening and closing. The resignation that Frank Woollaston is likely to escape scot free, with the mystery of what happened this weekend a long way from being solved.

Sleep well, Detective. Fingers crossed you wake up at the other end of it...

THE END

Go to p.293 to read your performance review.

148

'I presume these odds aren't serious,' you say to Susanna as you read down the list.

'Not really,' she agrees. 'But people have been taking this competition very seriously,' she adds.

'I'm not surprised with the prize money involved.'

'It is a bit much, isn't it?'

'Just a bit. I did ask at the committee but we were told the decision had already been taken.'

'Not the most democratic of committees?'

'You could say that.'

You read the list again: Heidi McLeish and North Castle are the favourites. Elaine Deandy and Old Norton second favourites? Well, they won't be winning now. But it's the name at the bottom that intrigues you. Peter Maddock and Little Norton are listed as the

100/1 outsiders here. It does seem that nobody thought he was going to win: apart from himself. Why?

Susanna has no insight to offer there, and you're aware that it's nearly time for the judges to meet and announce the top three.

But with everyone else distracted by the judging, might this be a moment to have a look around Peter Maddock's house? Head there via **184**.

Or should you head off to the village hall for the announcement? That's at **63**.

149

You let Veronica take the lead as you agree to follow her to the Midsomer coroner's office. You tell her that it would be good to follow her because you don't know the way, but part of you also wants to make sure she doesn't make any detours.

You also take the opportunity to call the station and update them. DS Lambie corroborates the fact that Peter Maddock was regarded as something of a loner. He was leading his village's entry into the weekend's competition, but there was no sense that anybody ever went out of their way to have a conversation with him. He kept himself to himself. No family either. At least, none that anyone seems to know about.

DS Lambie is heading over to the crime scene to see what he can discover. You might want to head over there once you're done with the coroner, he suggests.

For now, though, you make your way along the windy lanes and arrive at your destination. Veronica is speeding ahead a little, you notice, and you're struggling to keep up with her. Eventually, though, she slows in the distance. She appears to be talking – is she on the phone to someone? Your cars pull up outside the bland-looking brick building and you jump out, not quite knowing what horror is going to greet you inside.

Do you want to ask her whether she was making a call?
Go to **75**.
Or head straight in to the coroner's? Time might be of the essence. Go to **23**.

150

You're not sure anybody's had any cause to check out Peter Maddock's birth certificate for a while, but you also figure it's probably your only chance of finding out who his father is. That said, if Monica Davies wanted to keep the information under wraps, then that's likely how it'll stay.

But what if she didn't, you ponder as you put in the call for the information? What if she didn't want to cover up the mystery of her son, but felt that she had to? Might she at least leave some kind of clue if she wasn't about?

You nervously await the return call, conscious that this might be the moment that makes or breaks your investigation.

After what feels like hours, but is actually around 15 minutes, your phone bursts back into life. You snatch at it and take the call, listening agog as a revelatory piece of information is relayed to you. It turns out that your suspicion was correct.

On his birth certificate, Monica Davies didn't hide who the father of Peter Maddock was from anyone, if they chose to look. But who would?

The father field wasn't left empty. Instead, there was a name.

Frank Woollaston. The same Frank Woollaston who was married to Veronica. The very same Frank Woollaston who died nearly 20 years ago.

You tell DS Lambie the news, and he's even more shocked than you. 'Do you think Veronica knew?' you wonder.

'We could go and ask her and try and bring this to a close,' he says. 'Or maybe while she's still in hospital, we go and have a proper look at her house now we have something specific to go on?'

Go to the hospital and ask Veronica about the birth certificate. This should be fun. Over at **176**.
If she's in hospital, you can search her house, can't you? Try **163**.

151

Aware of the chatter from outside, you shift up a gear as you walk into the bedroom. A single bed that's unmade, but also doesn't show any sign of being slept in any time recently. There's a collection of clothes in the freestanding wooden wardrobe.

Not a lot of expense has been spent on furnishing the house, that much is clear. It's got the bare essentials, and not much of it looks brand new. Someone's second home, perhaps?

The bedside cabinet has nothing in it – not even a good detective book for bedtime – so you turn your attention to the wardrobe. There's a little cardboard box hiding behind a suitcase at the bottom of it. Just a handful of greetings cards inside, not much else. Still, you scoop up the contents and slip them into your inside pocket.

It's time to head back outside – the conversation is getting louder. How do you want to handle this?
Go out the front door of the house and call DS Lambie over?
Go to **58.**
Head out the way you came and walk over to the discussion that's taking place – that's **194.**

152

You continue walking along the small path and quickly become aware that it's curving around. It seems to wrapping its way behind the house. It takes about five minutes to walk the full length of it, but when it meets another lane, you recognize where you are instantly: back on the main road. Looking to your right, you see Veronica Woollaston's house in the distance. Mind you, it's a useful way to sneak away unnoticed, too, you think. But it's not got you any further in the investigation.

Do you want to go back and take a look at the car?
That might be worth a try at **133.**
Or track down the first officer who was on the scene?
They're over at **136.**
Or you could go back and try that gate after all? You need **28.**

153

Heidi McLeish doesn't answer her phone particularly quickly, but just as you fear it's about to click on to voicemail, an out-of-breath voice offers a harried 'Hello?'

'Heidi McLeish?' you ask, introducing yourself. 'John, load all those into the car,' she yells. She turns her attention back to you. 'Sorry, we're already running late. I just need to get my husband moving. He needs a quick kick to get him going in the morning.'

The pair of you agree to meet quickly at the café in North Castle. The judges aren't due in the village until noon, but she says she's got a long list of jobs she still needs to do.

You make sure to arrive promptly, and the two of you soon find yourself seated and in conversation. 'I was so sorry to hear about Peter,' she says earnestly. 'He didn't deserve that. Well, nobody deserves that.'

'Did you know him?'

'Not really, I'm afraid. I've long since learned to keep myself to myself around here. I occasionally pop my head above the parapet for a competition like this, but I'm afraid I'm a fan of the quiet life, Detective.'

'Nothing wrong with that,' you smile. 'A Sunday night in with a glass of wine and a good television drama is my idea of bliss.'

She smiles and relaxes. Over the course of the next 15 minutes you learn that she and John moved to North Castle around five years ago. The pair of them aren't short of money, 'Which is a good job,' she admits.

'Why so?'

'Our old house has stayed on the market for quite a while now,' she says. 'For some reason, we can't seem to shift it.'

'How long has it been up for sale?'

'Well, we first put it on the market seven years ago, but we've had to leave it empty for five.'

'Do houses usually take some time to sell around here?' you ask.

'They take a while. They're, er, not always on the cheap side. Still, we've not had a lot of interest.'

'Where is your old house?'

'Old Norton,' she says.

Old Norton. That's where Veronica lives, you quickly think. Heidi McLeish is ahead of you.

'I'd imagine you're well aware of Veronica Woollaston,' she says. 'Our old house is the one opposite. Turns out nobody was in a rush to live opposite the house where the man who got chewed up by a lawnmower lived. Can't say I was that keen either. Always some kind of drama going on over there.'

'Is that why you left? Were you around when he died?'

'Yes it was, and yes I was. Awful day. All very quick. Lots of visitors the night before too. Remember it as clear as yesterday.'

An alarm sounds from her phone. 'I'm so sorry, Detective,' she says. 'I'm going to have to go. I need to finish getting everything ready.'

You ask her to make sure she's available again if you need to talk to her, and wish her luck.

'Good luck to you too, Detective. I hope you catch whoever's done this.'

So do I, you think to yourself. So do I. Your train of thought is suddenly interrupted by an urgent message cropping up on your phone. *Find it at* **158.**

154

You bang at the door again, a little louder this time. 'I'm coming.' A firm, harried-sounding voice. It takes another minute before you hear the bolt on the other side of it being released.

The door is yanked open and a none-too-impressed woman is staring at you.

'Couldn't you just wait? Not everyone can get to the door quickly,' she snaps.

You haven't got off to a good start here, getting a dose of Veronica Woollaston's infamous sharpness already. You hold up your new identification card and introduce yourself.

'I'm afraid I've got some bad news,' you tell her. 'Would it be possible to come in?'

'What is it?'

'Do you know a Peter James Maddock?'

She pauses for a second.

'No, I'm afraid I don't recognize that name.'

That's odd, you think. But what do you do?

Do you thank her for her time, and leave? Go to **20.**
Or do you insist that she ask you inside? Head to **129.**

155

It's a brainwave, and a good one. There's a camera in this computer somewhere, and it's broadcasting. You don't immediately spot it. Thankfully, Peter Maddock didn't have one of those new-fangled computers where everything is built in. Instead, you follow a wire up to a shelf alongside you and spot the device. You angle it quickly towards the door of the little office room as you hear more movement downstairs.

That's odd, you think. Whoever it is appears to be looking for something. Don't they know you're up here? If they don't, then that means the person who you've just been chatting to isn't the person who's currently on the floor below you. Or were they just trying to distract you?

You pull up the list of contacts on Maddock's chat program. Who can you broadcast the call to? You need someone who can see it – and surely everyone will be at the judging by now?

You need to pick a name. But which of these on Maddock's contact list is it going to be? You narrow the choice down to...

Trevor Webber? Go to **138**.
Veronica Woollaston? Go to **3**.
Monica Davies? Go to **56**.

156

You throw down the headset and head for the exit, glancing out of the window as you do so. Where's the uniformed officer gone, you wonder? No time to find out as you storm down the stairs and head to the front door. You try the handle, taking a deep breath.

It's still unlocked. Thank goodness. You spot the uniformed officer in the distance and quickly head to your car. You're rattled, and behind the curve. You need to get back to Norton, you figure. Get back to where the competition is coming to a close.

As you approach the car you double-check the tyres. You don't know why, just instinct. It doesn't look like anybody's tampered with anything. You glance around. A few houses in the distance, sure, but nobody about, although you're conscious of the many windows looking down over the picturesque surroundings. Could whoever this person is be behind one of them?

And do you need to check that out? Looking at your watch, you realize you'll miss the competition's finale if you don't move. But maybe this is where you should be?

Do you head over to Norton and see how the competition plays out? Head to **63**.
Or is now the time to scout around Little Norton and see if you can find the mystery caller? Head to **39**.

157

You head back over to Mr Thomas. 'Dial it again, please,' you ask. He's not going to argue, no matter how unhappy he is about it.

He hits the redial button. This time, though, there's a flat tone at the other end of the line.

'Engaged?'

'Nobody's answering,' he says. 'It's not the engaged tone either.'

'Try again.'

He nods, and hits redial. This time, the sound is very, very slightly different. 'It's as if it rings for half a second, and then it's hung up straight away.'

'He's dumped the phone,' you say to DS Lambie.

'Broken the SIM card?'

'Can't be sure, but he's certainly not coming here.'

You walk over to the uniformed officers. 'False alarm. I think we scared whoever it is off.'

They head back to their vehicles as you go back to DS Lambie and talk tactics.

'Well, we definitely can't break in,' he says. 'We can get a search warrant for it, but that won't come through for a few hours at least.'

'Can't we sneak in and have a look?'

'Not a chance. We've just had uniformed officers here and the station knows where we are. I think we're out of leads.'

You kick the kerb in frustration, just as a call comes in from the Chief Inspector. You can't put this off any longer – you need to go back to the station.

Leaving DS Lambie in Bunbury, you reluctantly head back for your meeting. You sense this might be over. Go to **80.**

158

The message must have been urgent, as your phone beeps again before you get a chance to read the first alert. Even then, you need to read your screen twice. It's DS Lambie: he's been hurt.

You rush to your car and dial the station. You're quickly through to the Chief Inspector, who brings you up to speed.

'I've got a bad feeling about this,' he admits. 'I can assure you it's not a frequent occurrence that one of my officers is injured in the line of duty.'

Get to the point, you think.

'He's going to be okay. He'd only just got to Little Norton when he got another call,' he tells you.

'What did the call say?'

'It was from Elaine Deandy, over in Old Norton. Someone vandalized their display overnight. Some form of fast-acting weedkiller, it looks like. Only not used on weeds. Used on the floral displays.'

You try and process the two pieces of information at once. 'Lambie was hurt in Little Norton?' you ask.

'As he was leaving. He'd gone for a look around the crime scene with fresh eyes. Asking questions about the competition, the committee, that sort of thing.'

'Did he find anything?'

'You'll have to ask him that yourself. He wants to speak to you.'

'Where is he?'

'They've taken him to the doctor over there,' the Chief Inspector says.

'When do you think the display was sabotaged, sir?'

'Good question. Someone's just heading down there now. But it must have been either a very fast weedkiller or one that's impossible to detect.'

'I'd ask who would want one of the favourites knocked out of the competition, but...'

You don't even need to finish the sentence. But what you do need to do is decide where to focus your enquiry next.

Talk to DS Lambie at **87**.

Go and survey the damage in Old Norton at **139**.

159

You're not convinced. Ten minutes ago, Polly Monk was protesting her complete innocence. Now you learn that she's not as innocent as she makes herself sound.

What else might she confess?

'With respect, Ms Monk, if you were willing to sabotage one village's entry, how can't I be sure you're not involved with the sabotage of another?'

She looks shocked at the question.

'Are you seriously linking me with the death of Peter Maddock?'

'I'm just trying to eliminate people from the enquiry. How can I be sure?'

'Look, I told you what I did. I'm not proud of it. But that's a long way away from killing a man.'

She has a point. Still, you press on.

'A man is dead because of this competition.'

'Perhaps you should be asking those who seek to benefit from his death, then,' she spits. 'I can't believe this.' She's holding back tears. Either way, you've not won yourself a friend here.

She sits down, broken. 'This village. It all changed when those two moved in.'

'Which two?'

'Frank and Veronica Woollaston. This used to be such a lovely place to live. Right up until he died. It all changed after that.'

'What happened?'

'He died at the right time for her, that's what happened. I wouldn't wish it on anybody, but it solved her financial problems for a start. All those two used to do was row about money. Then she got her hold on the committee and here we are. It all changed then.'

What do you remember of his death? To ask that, go to **203**.
Hang on: if she was that unhappy with Veronica, why did she never stand against her? Ask that at **132**.

160

'Tell me about Polly Monk.'

Heidi McLeish gives you a cold, hard stare. A protracted silence. 'The cheating cow,' she eventually mutters.

'How is she cheating, exactly? From what I can tell, the Church Fields display was one of the best.'

'She knows something, Detective. I'm sure of that.'

'Know what?'

'You didn't see her face when the announcement was made, did you? I was watching her.'

'What were you looking for?'

'Exactly what I got when Old Norton was announced on the shortlist. Let's just say she doesn't play her cards very close to her chest. She looked the most surprised person there.'

'But she's not from Old Norton? She's from Church Fields.'

'Yet she knew that Old Norton was going to have the best display. And I think she did something about it.'

'What?'

'You must have heard the row and the door-slamming from the village hall. I'd bet they were talking about the sabotage. That, or money. They like arguing about that.'

The judges and committee had done their best to cover up the news that the Old Norton display had been tampered with. Still, in villages like these, they had no chance.

You nod.

'Firstly, what a surprise that the sabotaged display still manages to get on the shortlist. I presume they can thank Mrs Woollaston for that, what with it being her village.'

'But she's not one of the judges, is she?'

Heidi McLeish laughs. 'And what bloody difference do you think that makes?'

You take the point. 'What I don't understand is where Polly Monk fits into all of this?'

'Well, someone had to sabotage Old Norton.'

'Wait – and you think that was Polly?'

'Do you think it's not?'

'I'm asking you.'

'I saw her face, Detective. I've long suspected there's more to her than meets the eye. She always struck me as the sort to bend the rules at the best of times. But even if she didn't do it herself, I'm as certain as I can be that she knows somebody who knows something about it.'

She pauses for a minute, then gets into her car. 'I'm not difficult to find if you need anything else, Detective.'

Get back to the village hall. Head to **199**.
Go and find Polly Monk first. She's waiting for you at **41**.

161

What follows is quite the argument. It starts with Veronica reacting to Monica's bombshell, her quiet voice rising as she realizes her best friend has hidden the fact that she had a son all these years.

Monica blasts back. 'He's dead Veronica. Dead. My son. All because of your bloody flower competition. You had to have this competition, didn't you? You had to have such a huge amount of money for the top prize. Veronica knows best. Now look at us.'

She's silent. She's thinking. And then she says the words that'll ensure these two are never friends again.

'Was he Frank's?'

Frank? Frank Woollaston, her long-dead husband? The father of Peter Maddock?

Monica's pained look says more than words could. She doesn't even nod.

'Why didn't you tell me?' Veronica screams.

'How could I tell anyone? Frank threatened to kill me if I ever told anyone' Monica fires back.

Frank knew. Veronica is stunned into silence.

'And anyway, how could Peter have had any kind of life with all the gossips and backstabbers around here?'

'Is that aimed at me?' Veronica snaps back, her head spinning.

'Not just you. But the cap bloody well fits, doesn't it?'

'You're the one who had a child with my husband and never told me.'

'And look at why. You stole him off me in the first place.'

'Oh get over yourself, you jumped-up cow. You were his fling and you know it.'

'He wasn't short of those, was he? Couldn't wait to get away from you.'

'You were supposed to be my friend. I see right through you now,

Monica Davies. I'm only sad it's taken so long.'

'Well, you win as always, Veronica. That's the most important thing. Peter's dead now, so you don't have to worry about him, do you?'

You need to intervene here. What do you want to do?
You can separate them and let the result of the competition stand, bringing this whole charade to an end. *Go to* **142**.
Arrest the pair of them! *Head to* **54**.

162

You can't afford to take the chance. This man has murdered two people, you strongly suspect. You press the button to call a nurse and look him squarely in the eye.

'Frank Woollaston, I am arresting you for the...'

'Stop that, save your breath,' he says. 'I just needed to see her one last time, then I'll come quietly.'

'Why did you try to kill her?'

'I tried to *save* her,' he says, looking straight at you. 'She's the innocent party here. She always was. She only found out everything I was up to all those years ago when it was too late for her to stop it. By then, she'd put up with so much from me, I don't think she'd have tried to stop it anyway.'

'But why did you attack her?'

'Because if I hadn't, you'd have been questioning her in a police station by now. I couldn't risk you all thinking she was involved, that she was part of it. If she was in here, that gave her the right alibi.'

'She's hardly innocent.'

A nurse tries the door. He's locked it.

162

'Can we just have one minute?' he asks, adding a liberal dose of charm to his voice.

The nurse heads off. Either she's ceding to his request, or going off to get help. You hope it's the latter.

He turns back to you. 'She *is* innocent, Detective. She's not perfect, but then who is? Say what you like about my wife, but she wouldn't hurt a soul.'

Veronica is stirring, and her eyes open. 'Frank,' she gasps.

He turns his attention to her. Your head starts to thump.

'V,' he says. 'I wanted to tell you that I'm sorry, and I love you. I really do.'

She looks at him, both scared and clearly in love with him.

'But I have to say goodbye now,' he continues. 'I just needed to see you one last time.'

He gets up to leave and you go to follow suit. Your head is pounding, though. Your legs don't feel as strong. It's slightly harder to breathe, you think. Nonetheless, you stand, then collapse back down onto the chair. As you do so, Frank Woollaston kisses his wife on the top of her head as she drifts in and out of sleep, and quietly exits the room.

Your eyes start to close as a nurse runs in, alerted by the loud clatter as you fall to the floor. The tea, you realize. He's poisoned your cup of hospital tea. As if the stuff didn't taste bad enough already.

As you try desperately to catch your breath, you hope it's not the level of dose that killed Monica Davies. You certainly hope it's not anything as lethal as frog poison.

But even as you ponder that, and the medical staff try to revive you, Frank Woollaston gets into small, cluttered car and drives away from Midsomer for the last time. As he goes, he takes any chance of catching the killer with him...

THE END

Go to p.293 to read your performance review.

163

With Veronica Woollaston in hospital, you're hoping that there's still an officer at her house as you head on over, so you can at least have a look around. Thankfully, you're in luck. There's a police car parked outside.

For a village that tends to be light on traffic, you're surprised to see a small vehicle parked just out of sight of the main road as you approach. Interesting: the only house the owner could be visiting would be Veronica's or the one opposite her. Might be nothing, of course.

What do you want to do here? Do you want to go and examine the car, or head into Veronica's house to see what clues you can gather?

To examine the car, pop over to **198.**
If you're going to the house, you need **212.**

164

As it turns out, Susanna Swann isn't far away. She's been in charge of collating the entries and doing the administration for the competition, and when you get hold of her on the phone she's driving to Norton. You ask if she can park just outside the village so the pair of you can have a quiet word.

You know that she runs a café in Hayley Green. 'She's our newest committee member,' Veronica told you as she gave you her number. 'We needed some young blood.'

When you see her pull up in her car, her mane of white hair does lead you to question just what Midsomer's idea of young is, but you opt not to press the point. Instead, you introduce yourself. She's quickly efficient and a little abrupt. Still, if you fell out with everybody who's abrupt around here...

The clock's ticking, so you get down to business and quiz her about the committee as you stand outside your cars. You appreciate that the pair of you might just be in a vulnerable spot here – you never know who could drive past and see you talking – but figure it'd cause too much alarm to do something about that now.

Instead, you start asking a few questions about the events of the last 24 hours, and note that Susanna gets less sure when the subject of the committee is brought up. 'They're a friendly bunch, really, but they do scare me a bit. Me being the young one and all.'

Turns out that as the designated young person, she's in charge of the committee's Facebook group. It felt quite an advanced idea when she first proposed it a few years ago – there was some resistance after how MySpace worked out for them – but it's proven useful over time for people around Midsomer to keep in light touch with each other.

She confesses she's been worried by one or two of the messages she sees, though.

'What kind of messages?'

'Nothing abusive,' she quickly steadies herself. 'Just, well, things like "you lot should be ashamed of yourselves" and "you've ruined the area". Usual internet rubbish.'

'Aimed at the committee?'

'Yes,' she nods.

'Can I see this group?'

'Well, this phone is a bit old, but it just about works,' she says, pulling it out of her bag. She loads the page up and lets you scroll through the discussion. One name stops you in your tracks: Peter Maddock.

'Did he post often?'

'A little bit. But I should show you this.'

Her fingers swipe and prod the screen and she pulls a list of odds someone's put together for who'll win the weekend's competition. There's some discussion underneath, and a dispute over Heidi McLeish and North Castle being listed as the favourites. 'Over my dead body,' Maddock wrote. 'Or yours'.

The pair of you stare at the message. You're not short of questions.

Ask Susanna about Heidi McLeish. Why would Peter Maddock not want her to win? Go to **88.**
Who came up with the odds? Let's find that out at **148.**

165

No time to lose here. You duck into the small study room. It's not particularly well kept, and could use a spring clean. A basic, not very convincingly assembled flatpack desk sits in the corner of the room, and there's a pile of ring binders just to the side of it.

You flick through the binders as quickly as you can. Bank statements, dating back to the start of the year. What's more, they're not Monica Davies' or Peter Maddock's bank statements. They're the statements for the village committee. Of course: Monica would have overseen its finances as part of her role there.

You quickly leaf through them, but realize you're going to need more time to examine them. Hurriedly, you rip them out of the binder and put them in your inside pocket. You're very aware, though, that you're needed outside, and you head out to find DS Lambie deep in conversation with Mr Thomas.

'DS Lambie,' you call across, heading towards your car.

He looks up.

'We've got to go – we've had an urgent call from the station.'

With Mr Thomas distracted, Lambie takes advantage of the exit you've offered and heads towards you.

'Get in your car and find somewhere down the road where we can talk,' you say through gritted teeth. 'Do it quickly, he's still filming us.'

Lambie scurries to his car and you follow suit, following him as he drives back out of Bunbury and eventually pulls into a secluded layby five minutes down the road. You get out of your cars and are soon in conversation.

'Was Mr Thomas okay?' you check.

'Don't know. He wasn't happy. He was watching that house for a reason, and I just hope that doesn't come back to bite us.'

'Not much we can do about it now. But we can do something about this.'

You hold out the collection of bank statements you took from the house, just as your phone starts to ring.

'It's the Chief Inspector,' you tell Lambie.

'You'd better answer it, he doesn't tend to ring for social calls.'

It's up to you. Answer the call? That's **48.**
Ignore it, and prioritize the statements. Go to **208.**

166

'Mr Thomas,' you say, allowing a little exasperation into your voice. 'I'm here as part of a murder enquiry.'

A flash of worry across his eyes. 'I–I don't know anything about that,' he says. Suddenly, the hard exterior he's been putting across is softening fast. You suspect he's just who he says he is: a man who's been given a bit of money to keep an eye on things, but with no desire to get into trouble.

'You are not a suspect, Mr Thomas. But I need to know who is paying you to watch this house.'

'You think that woman and her son are murderers?'

'No. They've both been murdered. Murdered in the last 48 hours. And there's a killer out there somewhere. I'll ask you again: who have you sent that photograph to?'

'I'm not sure of their names.'

'Wait, there are two people?'

'Well, yeah. There used to be. Peter used to slip me a few quid, but he hasn't for a while.'

The other person?

'He introduced himself as John. I couldn't tell you if that's his real name. I've only seen him once, and that was years ago. But he makes sure the money comes through every few months. I just have to message him if I see anyone going into the house.'

'Have you seen anyone recently?'

'Nobody's been near it for some time now.'

'Do you have that number?'

He hands it over. 'I don't know nothing about any murders, though,' he says again. He's very keen to get this across.

DS Lambie pulls in as your conversation comes to an end. You quickly bring him up to speed, and ponder your options. Do you press ahead with investigating the house? Go to **64**. *Or are you going to follow up on the number that Mr Thomas has given you? You need* **37**.

167

'I really could use seeing that typewriter, I'm afraid. I just need to make sure I cover everything off.'

'Very well,' Geoff Webber says, his hospitable mood evaporating pretty quickly. It suddenly strikes you that the shed is going to be towards the bottom of his garden, and you'll be going there alone with him. You hadn't planned on how exposed that's going to make you, but still: you follow him down a long path towards the shed.

To call it a shed, though? Well, this is a Webber shed. It's bigger than the flat you used to live in, you think. He switches the lights on as he steps inside, and you're thankful it's well lit. It takes him just a few seconds to find the typewriter, and it's instantly clear that his story stacks up. You haven't made a friend here, but at least you can rule the Webbers out of your enquiries for now.

'I trust that'll be all,' says Geoff Webber, guiding you towards the front door.

'Thank you very much for your time,' you say with as much earnestness as you can muster. You head back into your car, over to your hotel and call it a night. Tomorrow's fun starts on **69**.

168

If you were a little cautious when pulling in to the drive of Veronica Woollaston's impressive house the first time around, your senses are doubly alert the second. Where on earth could she have gone? And perhaps more importantly, why did she take off like that without telling you she was leaving?

Her long gravel drive betrays no sign of fresh tyre tracks apart from your own. As you step out of your car, you check the little post box at the front of her house. A couple of bills, a leaflet for an archery club. Nothing unusual or suspicious. You approach the front door and knock, but this time nobody comes and lets you in.

It feels like a dead end.

Feeling defeated, you're heading back to the car when your detective instincts kick in. You cautiously creep around to the side of the house, and over the low fence you see that a gate is slightly ajar. Through it, you see the extensive vegetable garden, which seems undisturbed. A pond lies in the now-baking sun at the back of the garden, with a few frogs looking content at the edge. A collection of croquet hooks are ready for a quick knock around, too.

And then you notice it: the back door to the house. A very slight tickle of wind confirms what you thought you'd spotted, as the door slowly rocks back and forth.

It's open.

Why is it open? You don't have time to consider that before your phone bursts into life. A message: get to Little Norton as quickly as possible. If you don't examine the scene of death quickly, it's going to be even more disturbed.

It's your choice, Detective... You don't have anything as convenient as a warrant – but who's going to mind if you take a quick look inside the house? Go to **93**.

No: you need to get to that murder scene now. Drive over to Little Norton by heading to **84**.

169

'I'm very sorry, Mr Woollaston. The law doesn't work like that. You both have questions to answer here.'

'Then *I'm* very sorry, Detective. I can't let that happen. You can arrest me. But not my wife.'

You reach for your phone and start to call the station. Frank Woollaston closes the gap between him and you and furiously knocks the phone out of your hand. 'I said I can't let that happen.' He's not being so quiet and reasonable now.

'Please don't provoke him,' Veronica says, fear in her voice. She's seen this side of him before.

The two of you exchange a quick glance. You're in trouble here, and you know it. Frank goes across to your phone and stamps on it for good measure.

'Frank, you can't do this. You can't,' Veronica says, trying to appeal to him. For a minute he considers this, but he's read the situation a little better than her. He knows he has very few ways out here.

He walks back towards you, his face losing its steel for a minute. 'I didn't want this. I never wanted this. I just wanted her to be okay.' He gestures at Veronica, her face a mix of love and fear.

You survey the room, looking for exits, searching for anything to defend yourself with. There's a croquet set in the other room, but you'll never get to it. Likewise, you remember Veronica's walking stick by the front door. You've got two places you can head to from here: into the kitchen, or out into the hallway. Because if you stay here, you don't fancy your chances of making it back out of the room at all...

Go to the kitchen! That's **15.**
No! Try the hallway! Go to **68.**

170

DS Lambie calls through the front door as he continues to knock, but you ask him to give you a few minutes. He heads back to Monica Davies' house next door. Your attention remans on Hazel.

'Did Monica Davies have any allergies you know of? Any underlying health problems?'

'Nothing she mentioned. Neither of us is young, Detective, but apart from when she had that fall, and the odd cold, she's as fit as a fiddle. An old fiddle, but still a fiddle.'

You sit and ponder for a minute. 'There's no underlying health problem. And the key to her house has been taken from yours.'

'You could check with the doctor, I suppose? She might know something.'

You know that someone's already checked Monica's medical records, and found nothing. It doesn't seem as though Hazel can add much here.

'We do that as routine,' you say, impatiently.

Hazel O'Brien crumples into tears. 'I can't believe she's gone. I just can't believe it.'

Her sobs grow louder and soon she's inconsolable. You get little sense that she's been involved in any way with Monica's death. But that key? That's niggling you.

DS Lambie's back. You leave Hazel behind for the moment, calling for another officer to sit with her. In the meantime, DS Lambie has some important news: the working theory now is that Monica Davies was poisoned. Her dentures were poisoned.

You keep your expression emotionless until you step outside Hazel's house, but then the shock sinks in. Two murders? In two days? Just what is this place? And let's not forget that Veronica Woollaston is lying in a bed in Causton Hospital.

Go and have a look around Monica Davies' house in more detail at **90**.

Head over to Veronica. See if you get anywhere further with her? Find out at **181**.

171

You head to your car for the short journey over to Norton Green, hoping to catch Trevor Webber before the bustle of the day gets going. You check the address you've been given and park outside. The curtains are drawn. Your initial impression is that Mr Webber is not an early riser.

You ring the doorbell and finally hear some noise coming from the other side of it. To your surprise, Trevor Webber is quite a young man. Everyone else you've met in connection with this competition is, well, of a different age demographic. Here, though, is someone who doesn't even look out of his twenties.

'You're early,' he says, as he opens the door. You check your watch. Nine o'clock? You hold up your identification and the cocky smile that was on his face drops a little. Who was he expecting?

'You'd best come in,' he says, leading you in to his impressive but slightly unkempt house. 'You're thinking I'm too young for all of this, right?' he grins, regaining his composure.

'The thought had crossed my mind,' you admit, as he clears some discarded papers from a chair for you to sit down. He moves what looks like a broken typewriter or old computer from another and sits himself. He doesn't offer you a drink. 'I've done it for my parents really, just put my name on it all for them.'

'Your parents being?'

'The people who paid for the whole thing,' he grins. 'Geoff Webber? Alice Webber? Webbers' Inns?'

A pub chain. The biggest chain of village pubs in this part of the country, you realize.

'Are you not interested in the competition yourself?' you ask, bringing the conversation back on point.

'A little. I like that it winds them all up that I'm taking part.'

'Why does it wind them up?'

He laughs. 'Well, you must have noticed it yourself, Detective. I'm the only finalist who's not an absolute fuddy duddy! It drove them all mad when they saw my name on our village's entry form!'

'Did they not expect it?'

'I suppose,' he laughs. 'Mum and dad did pay for the committee, after all. Would have been rude to leave a Webber off the entry list.'

'What'll they do if you win?'

'I'm not that bad, Detective,' he guffaws. 'I've already had a quiet word. I'm not going to win. I just wanted to wind them all up. Seemed to work, too.'

Another knock at the door. Trevor Webber gets up. 'I hope you'll excuse me, Detective,' he smiles. 'This is the person I was hoping would be knocking on my door first thing today.'

You get up to leave and hand him your number. He assures you, although you're not sure you believe him, that he'll be in touch if he hears anything. You walk past a young woman on the doorstep. You sense that Trevor Webber might be grateful that his village is last on the judge's timetable for the day.

As you head back to the car, your phone buzzes: an urgent message. And it's not even 10 o'clock yet.
You can check it at **158**.

172

There's nothing much of note about the grave, you reason. Hopefully, someone around here will at least remember the funeral. You head to the main church building in the centre of the grounds. It's an old, beautiful and welcoming place, and the doors are open. The sign as you walk in invites visitors to come in for a silent prayer. A donation box is at the door, too.

What there isn't, though, is a vicar.

But then this is competition weekend. It's not likely they'd have any weddings to officiate on the same day as the Villages In Bloom competition. You get the impression that the already-infamous committee would have seen to that.

You take a look at the signs and notices posted around the church as you step inside, but find nothing fresh. You walk down to the front and tentatively knock at a door set to the side. It's quite a big building, and you figure there must be a room or two tucked away here. Again, no sign of anyone about as you tap the door, and it's firmly locked. The church must just be left open during the day.

You turn back and figure you'd best get going. You head back to the main door, and see that it's swung shut while you've been at the other end of the church.

And then you realize: it hasn't just swung shut. It's not the wind pushing it to and fro. Somebody has closed it.

More than that, somebody has just locked you in.

What do you do? Call for help? Try to make a phone call?
Go to **79.**
Or do you try to make your way out through the door at the other end of the church? Head to **173.**

173

You figure that, what with the competition arranged for this weekend and all church occasions cancelled, there's not much chance of anyone casually walking by to hear your cry for help even if you screamed at the top of your lungs. Furthermore, the only person you assume who's in the vicinity is whoever's just bolted you into this church. They need no further invitation to come for you.

You need to move, and you need to move fast.

It's quite a big church, you realize, as you zip back towards the door offset to the side. It's firmly closed, but this door looks less substantial than the one at the main entrance. You push hard at it, and feel it budge a little. Looking around, you see no other obvious way out. What you then definitely make out is a sound coming from the other side of this door. Whoever's locked you in the church appears to have gone round to another entrance, and seems to be heading towards you via this door.

How do you want to play this?
Do you want to charge at the door and break it down, hopefully to get past whoever's coming your way? Go to **45**.
Or do you hide in the open church, and try and gain the upper hand? Go to **213**.

174

As you edge forward towards the exact spot where Peter Maddock's body was found, you're conscious of the shards of glass near where you're standing. They crunch a little under your feet and you stop to take in the scene. From what you can tell, the murderer was unlikely to have come from Maddock's house – more likely, they made their way over the fence and approached from the rear of the property.

The garden is much bigger than you'd expect for the house it's set behind. Although it's not the largest property you've seen in the area, you figure the garden alone means it's not cheap to maintain. He must have sold a lot of damson jam.

Looking further, you figure that that someone could easily have approached without Maddock being aware of them.

That said, you're seeing little that contradicts the working theory. It's unlikely the jars of jam themselves would have ended his life, but the combination of those with the heavy shelves? That seems to make sense. Still, the perpetrator must have a bit of strength to them, not just to shift those shelves, but to do so with enough momentum to crush someone underneath.

Another thought too: there doesn't seem to have been a huge struggle here, or at least there's certainly no sign of one. But those shelves don't look like they'd have moved without some force. That leads you to one of two theories. Either the attacker managed to get inside the greenhouse without being noticed, or perhaps Maddock recognized them?

Your next stop? Well, the Midsomer village committee is gathering together at the village hall in Norton. They want to know if their competition is still going ahead. You can head there now by going to **35.**

Or feel free to look around the rest of the garden, over at **186.**

175

Frank Woollaston looks at the phone in your hand.

'Hang it up,' he says. This time you do so. It's heard enough, after all.

As far as Frank Woollaston is concerned, you've got enough on him now. Whoever was on the other side of that phone call has the information on him they need.

Even if he were to attack you, that person knows he's alive, and will open an investigation: an investigation that would likely see Veronica Woollaston brought in for questioning too. That's the last thing Frank wants.

Thankfully for you, what Frank doesn't know is that the phone went to a random number. That you bashed the keys as best you could in the middle of your struggle, but ended up dialling a complete stranger. You don't have any incentive to tell him that, of course, and you know you have to project absolute confidence, lest he suspect otherwise.

For the moment, you have a huge advantage.

'You're looking very well for a dead man, Mr Woollaston.'

He looks broken and crouches to the ground, trying to compose himself. He starts to cry.

'We were broke,' he eventually blurts out. 'We needed the money.'

'We being you and Veronica?'

He nods. 'You don't understand. All we ended up doing was fighting about money. We could barely cover the mortgage and, well, you've seen Veronica. She doesn't exactly go for the cheaper things in life.'

'Whose idea was it?'

'Mine, I suppose. I only wanted the best for her. I couldn't find anything else I hadn't tried.'

'How did you do it?'

'Peter,' he whispered. He explained how Peter Maddock had arranged everything under the cover of one of his amateur dramatics shows. A life-size dummy, some professional make-up effects. And, of course, a hefty pile of banknotes to a coroner with one eye on retirement. A few other details needed to be sorted, of course, he explains. But everybody bought it: after all, who wouldn't? It's not like Midsomer is some kind of crime capital.

He snuck back in more and more over the years, taking advantage, over the past four or five years, of the empty house opposite Veronica's. There were a few close calls, but he managed to evade suspicion. Life went on. Until Peter Maddock started to get greedy. He'd make calls to Frank from his computer demanding more and more money. Until, well, it just got too much.

'You know I have to arrest you?'

He nods. 'I'll tell you the rest of what happened. Just let me go and get my bag from in there.'

You nod. You assume that he's going to confess to Peter Maddock's murder, to tell you who else was involved and how, and that'll bring the whole sorry business to an end. You're exhausted, and it's only as he goes to get his belongings that you realize how close this all came to falling apart.

Your thoughts are disturbed by a sharp yell.

Oh no.

You run back through the small door on the outside of the church to see Frank Woollaston on the floor, looking at you.

'I'm sorry, Detective,' he gasps. 'At least you have the recording. I–I just need to protect my Veronica one last time.'

You look down as the blood gushes from his wrists. You race towards him to try and stop the bleeding, but he's dug too deep. There's nothing you can do.

In the days that follow, you get pats on the back at the station, and people are genuinely shocked at Frank Woollaston's reappearance.

But it's just your word. The phone call went to thin air. None of his confession was recorded. It's assumed that he was behind the death of Peter Maddock, but he too isn't around to tell his side of the story.

A partial victory, you tell yourself. There's more you could have done here, but it's been quite an adventure your first few days in Midsomer.

'Is it always like this, Sarge?' you ask DS Lambie.

He smiles. 'Come on, I'll buy you a drink.'

THE END

Go to p.293 to read your performance review.

176

There's a lot to make sense of here, and not many people to help you do so. The one person who knew Monica Davies and Frank Woollaston? Well, she's lying in a hospital bed, having been attacked herself. But who else can you talk to about this?

You and DS Lambie look at each other. 'I'll go,' you say. 'You see if you can dig up anything back at the station.'

When you arrive at the hospital this time, you feel a sense of dread; you've no idea how Veronica is going to react. She's certainly looking like her world has collapsed as you walk in to her room and find her awake. She's staring into nowhere, a cup of watery-looking tea abandoned to the side of her. She's still hooked up to machines, but seems to be a bit more with it.

Inevitably, she's not particularly pleased to see you. Well, you assume that, but this time she barely acknowledges your presence as you enter the room.

How do you want to approach this? She knows what's going on! Assume that and get questioning at **185**.
Or how about playing dumb? You need **130** *if that's your approach.*

177

Trevor Webber is representing Norton Green, you remember. You're sure you saw a stall from there among the tables selling local produce. Maybe they know something? It doesn't take you long to find it: a little table with some exceptionally tasty-looking shortbread for sale.

'Want some?' asks the woman sitting behind it. You'd guess she's in her early forties and, judging by how full her table is, she's not had a lot of custom today. You dig out a few coins and purchase a biscuit in the shape of a star.

'Delicious,' you smile.

'You're the new detective, aren't you?'

'That's right. I see you're from Norton Green?'

'Only lived there for two years, though. I'm the outsider,' she laughs. 'Judith Langan. Nice to meet you.'

'Fancy your chances in the Villages In Bloom competition?'

'I can't say I've had much involvement in it. That's Trevor Webber's department. Well, him and his parents.'

'I didn't think his parents lived in the village?'

'They don't, but that's not stopped them having their say.' She looks at you and lowers her voice a little. 'Half of Norton Green can hear those three arguing when they get going.'

'Have you seen him today? Doesn't appear to be here?'

'I think they're all in the village hall.'

'Not sure they are, a few people haven't arrived yet.'

'Well, Trevor was certainly here a little while ago. I saw him talking to Polly. Not a friendly chat either by the looks of it.'

'Any idea where he might have gone?'

'Check if his car's in the car park. You can't miss his number plate.'

Good idea, you think, as you demolish the rest of your shortbread. Still, just as you're munching it, that very car roars into the village.

You spot it as Trevor Webber parks up. What do you reckon? Worth a quick word with him? Go to **38.**
Or perhaps you should see if you can find out what Polly Monk has to say? Go to **218.**

178

You close the door behind you, leaving you and Veronica in the village hall together.

'Why is it worthless?' you ask her.

'Because there's no money,' she sobs. 'That's what the row was about earlier. We were told there are no funds left to pay the prize money.'

You look puzzled. 'Where's the £100,000 prize money gone, then?'

'The Webbers said they were going to plug any gaps in our finances. But they've refused. They want nothing more to do with the committee or the competition. We're ruined. I'm ruined.'

Ruined? Rumours have swirled all day that the area was short of money, and that Veronica was too. But here's the confirmation.

'Why do you need the money, Mrs Woollaston? What's so important?'

'It's £100,000, you idiot,' she snaps, losing control. She doesn't lose control very often, but when she does? Well, you can understand why people didn't like getting on the wrong side of her.

'That'd replace all the money I had to pay him.'

Hang on.

'Pay who?'

She's realized what she's said. She's also realized that she can't take it back. She mumbles something and tries to backtrack anyway, but you're not having it.

'Pay who, Mrs Woollaston?'

She looks broken.

'Pay who?'

'Peter,' she whispers. 'Peter.'

'Maddock?'

'I didn't kill him Detective. I really didn't.'

'Then who did?'

'Yes, who did?' Another voice.

You both turn around. Monica Davies is standing there. She must have been in one of the back rooms of the hall.

'I'm very sorry, I'm not sure what this has to do with you?'

'Peter Maddock was my son,' she says, with absolute steel in her eyes. 'And I want to know who killed him.'

Veronica's jaw drops. She has words she wants to say here. But do you let her?

Let Veronica and Monica have this out. Go to **161**.

Ask Monica what on earth she's going on about? Head to **54**.

179

You look at Veronica, her life seemingly falling apart around her. 'Mrs Woollaston, there's been some gossip that you've been struggling financially. Is there anything to that?'

She pauses, then gently nods her head.

'And now you've been threatened and attacked. Is any of this linked, Mrs Woollaston?'

A longer pause. You hold your breath as you wait for her answer. Her head nods again.

'I think you need to come clean with me, Mrs Woollaston.'

She finally takes a sip of the pale excuse for a cup of tea next to her, grimacing as it passes her taste buds.

'I was being blackmailed, Detective. Blackmailed. And I couldn't afford to pay anymore.' The tears go from a sob to a flood. 'I don't know what I'm going to do.'

A nurse passes by, to check everything is okay. Veronica nods, and they cautiously move away and leave you to it.

The story tumbles out, even as your phone continues to vibrate. Peter Maddock had been blackmailing her, and over the past year or two, his demands had been growing.

The cost of keeping two houses, you conclude. Selling damson jam at the farmer's market was unlikely to have given Maddock the income to cover that. But what did he have over her? He must have something to blackmail her to the point where she's running out of money?

'The Villages In Bloom competition? With the £100,000 prize money? I assume you were going to find a way to win that?'

'I–I'm sorry. I'm sorry. I needed to find a way to pay him off.'

'And did you kill him?'

'No!' She looks genuinely shocked.

'Do you know who did?'

'I–I think it was the same man who attacked me, Detective.'

'Do you have a name?'

She almost whispers it, she says it that quietly. But there's no mistaking the name that tumbles out of her lips.

'F–Frank.', she splutters. 'Frank. He was trying to... well, protect me, I think. To throw you off the scent...'

Frank Woollaston? Her husband? He's alive? Get that news to the station fast. Head to **11**.
Ha, you're not buying that! Arrest Veronica and get this wrapped up. Go to **74**.

180

You head back to the station and sit at your little-used desk. Gradually the case comes together. As the investigation winds down over the coming days, there's at least some partial closure.

The substance you found hidden away in the abandoned car was indeed poison. A deadly agent that'd been used to contaminate Monica Davies' dentures. Fibres from Monica's house – and it'd take a while to determine this – would match those found in Veronica's. It was harder among all the damsons and spilt jam to glean fibres from the scene of Peter Maddock's death, but the working theory is that all three crimes were linked.

Veronica Woollaston recovered, although the idea of another Villages In Bloom competition would be abandoned. Eventually, as her money ran out, she'd have to move elsewhere, but she'd long resigned from the committee by then anyway. The house opposite her would finally sell too, after years on the market. Some degree of normality would resume.

You'd continue to work at Midsomer CID, and come to call the place home. But you'd never get the satisfaction of solving your very first case.

Whoever it was who committed those terrible crimes, they're out there somewhere, perhaps even plotting the next one...

THE END

Go to p.293 to read your performance review.

181

You decide your best chance at getting anywhere here is with Veronica Woollaston. Even as you undertake the drive back to the hospital, you feel this is a long shot. You head back through the hospital, knocking softly on the door to her room and letting yourself in. She's a little bit more awake than last time you saw her, but still looking a shadow of her former self.

She sees you come in, but doesn't say anything.

You decide to go in soft. 'I'm so sorry about the news.'

She looks puzzled. And that's when you realize you may have miscalculated: Veronica doesn't know. 'What news?' she whispers.

'I'm so sorry, Mrs Woollaston. I'm afraid Monica Davies died this morning.'

Her face is a cocktail of shock, despair and sheer upset. Tears quickly, uncontrollably run down her face. 'No, no, no,' she sobs. 'Not Moni.'

You wait a minute, the intensity of the beeps from the machines surrounding Veronica increasing. A nurse comes in hurriedly to see what's happening.

'Are you okay, Mrs Woollaston?' she asks.

You reply for her. 'I'm afraid she's just had some very bad news.'

The nurse moves in to check Veronica. Her eyes are awash with tears.

'I know you need to ask your questions, Detective, but please: Mrs Woollaston still needs her rest.'

You nod, and quickly put a few questions to Veronica. Can she give them any leads on who attacked her? Does she think it was the same person who attacked Peter Maddock? Who can she think of who would have had an axe to grind against Monica Davies?

She's silent, shaking her head to your questions. She looks at you earnestly, a drop of humanity behind her usually steely exterior. 'Phillip someone,' she says. 'Smith, I think.' She gives you an address some distance away. 'Moni talked about him sometimes. I don't know if they were having a relationship, but I think they used to be close. Please tell him.'

She starts to doze back off to sleep, the painkillers taking effect. You feel you're running out of leads, and this is the only one you've got left. You need to head over to the mysterious address.
Go to **13.**

182

You listen to the Chief Inspector, and a sinking feeling grows in your stomach. If you go back, what if you're taken off the case? You're making progress here, and you'd rather have something substantive to go back with, not least because some of your methods haven't been quite how the Chief Inspector would expect things to be done.

You take a breath. 'I'm sorry, sir: I'm just following up a lead and I'm hoping I'll have some news in the next hour or two. Can I just see if this heads anywhere, and I'll come straight in afterwards?'

There's a pause on the line. 'What lead is it you're following up, Detective?'

'Can't quite say,' you gulp. 'Might be something, might be nothing, but I just need to quickly check something out.'

'You need to give me something to go on, Detective.' He didn't get to become Chief Inspector by rolling over that easily.

Realizing you need to tell him something, you throw him one of Monica Davies's bones. 'It turns out that Monica Davies has a past. I've found a link between her and Peter Maddock.'

He pauses again. He wants to support the new recruit, clearly, but he's fighting his own instincts a little. Still, he relents.

'I need progress by the end of the day, Detective. There are a lot of eyes on this case.' He hangs up.

You turn to DS Lambie. 'If we don't solve this case, I'll be spending the next six months behind a desk.'

'The Chief Inspector?'

You nod.

'What was the link between Davies and Maddock you were talking about?'

'I think they're related. I think they're mother and son,' you say, to his obvious surprise.

He takes a second. 'Go on.'

'Humour me, because I'm new around here. But if Peter Maddock was Monica's son, why would they hide that? It's not as if she was married or anything, and it's hardly the 1800s?'

He raises his eyebrows. 'It is around here.'

A wry grin on your face. 'Okay then, try these: why are they meeting at that house? Who actually owns it? And who was Peter Maddock's father?'

'I'm guessing the Chief Inspector wants answers quickly. Which of those leads do you want to follow?'

Run a search to see who owns the house: go to **40.**
Find out who's listed as the father on Peter Maddock's birth certificate? Search that on **150.**

183

It's firmly to your advantage, you figure, that whoever's in the house hasn't clocked you. Also, they appear to have got what they want, and are looking to get out of Peter Maddock's home a lot quicker than they got in.

You shuffle slightly forward, hoping to get some kind of vantage point. Perhaps to see who it is.

Although your angle is a little awkward and you can't make out their face, you do notice what they're wearing. It takes you aback just for a minute. Isn't that... a police uniform?

It appears to be. A police officer? Or just someone who's got hold of a uniform? A costume of some sorts? All good questions. But hang on: wasn't there a uniformed officer outside the house? That sinking feeling returns to your stomach as you wait for the intruder to leave. You hear them get to the bottom of the stairs, make a sharp turn and head out of the front door. They don't bother to close it. You race across to see if you can see anything out of the window. Sadly, all you can spot is a car moving away. Whoever it was has gone.

You head outside and see the uniformed officer in the distance. You approach them, but straightaway see that their build doesn't match that of the figure you just saw. It's not them. Maybe the officer let them in? It's a fleeting thought, but you soon dismiss it. The officer was over the other side, by the greenhouse. He wouldn't have seen anything, let alone heard anyone from there.

Still, you go and check.

'Anything?' you ask.

'Nothing,' the young constable replies. 'It's dead here,' he says, before correcting himself. 'I'm sorry, I didn't mean...'

'It's okay, Constable, don't worry.' You fill him in on what's happened, and he's shocked and was indeed oblivious. 'Keep a close eye on the area, just in case.' But you know in your heart of hearts that whoever it was has gone now.

You'd best go to Norton and find out how they're getting on with the competition. Hopefully, there'll be a clue you can follow up there. Get on over to **63**.

184

You're taking no chances as you get back into your car and decide to head over to Little Norton. You call the station and tell them where you're going. Thankfully, there should be a uniformed officer there this time, so you won't be alone. Still, you're not sure what to say when they ask why you're heading back over. Thankfully, when you tell them it's just a loose end you want to check on, they seem satisfied. It's not as if there's nothing else keeping the local police extremely busy.

So far, most of the investigation has centred on the greenhouse and garden area where Maddock was found. However, as an outsider, you're determined to find out a little bit more about him. As you pull up, you greet the uniformed officer and show your ID. They let you under the police tape that cordons the site off, and you make your way over to the main house. They head off to walk the garden again.

But what should you look for?

Is it worth rooting around to see if he has a laptop, a computer? Just something that'd connect him online. Mind you, out of the corner of your eye, you see a phone with an answering machine light blinking.

You reckon you've got a small window of time here before you need to move on. Where do you want to concentrate your energies?

That phone looks interesting. Check out the answerphone messages and see if there's anything of note. Go to **115**.
He must have a computer around here somewhere. Head upstairs and see if you can find it. Go to **8**.

185

You've come so far over the past couple of days that you simply don't see the point of tip-toeing around anymore. You've felt from the start of your time in Midsomer that Veronica has treated you with a little bit of contempt at best. She's certainly held back on her fair share of information.

Still, it's a gamble to assume that she knows everything you've discovered. A gamble, you calculate, worth taking.

'I know about Monica and your late husband.'

Her face drops. She'd not make much of a poker player, you quickly reason, her reaction confirming to you that this was a relationship she knew about too.

'And I know about Peter Maddock.'

This time she looks a little more puzzled. Interesting. Perhaps she's only got half the story here herself. Still, no point filling in the gaps for her until she's come clean with you.

'Perhaps you can tell me your side of events?'

She tries to recover her composure. 'I don't understand what Frank's past has got to do with this?'

'Mrs Woollaston, Monica Davies was murdered this morning.'

More shock. 'It was murder?'

You nod. Tears well up in her eyes again.

'Mrs Woollaston?'

'She was friends with Frank before me. They went to school together. Had a fling when they were younger, and then Monica went away for a few years when they broke up. She was devastated.'

'Were they still involved when you were married to Frank?'

She looks hurt at the question, but perhaps not because you've asked it. After a few seconds she quietly responds. 'No. Frank wasn't the most faithful husband. I could never talk to Monica about him. She always got too upset.'

'What do you mean when you say Frank wasn't the most faithful husband?'

'Just that,' she sighs. 'I tried to put on a front that it was all happiness. But he wasn't always a very nice person.'

This certainly goes against the impression you've been given so far. From what you've gleaned so far, Veronica was always the one who was hard work. Everybody seemed to love Frank.

If you want to turn the conversation to Peter, go to **105**.
Or ask about Frank's death at **46**.

186

Satisfied you're not going to glean anything else from the greenhouse itself, you take a look around the sizeable garden sitting behind Peter Maddock's tiny house. There's been a police presence here for several hours already, so it's long been determined that there are faint footprints that support the theory the attacker came over the fence at the back of the house, rather than from the front.

The other thing that strikes you is the floral work. Peter Maddock clearly spent a lot of time here. You've already seen glimpses as you drove here of the wonderful displays being set up for the Villages In Bloom competition. What you see around Maddock's garden are some beautiful blooms, but you can't help thinking they're not quite up to the very high standard of some of those others. Still, this has clearly been a labour of love.

You don't find any further clues, but you figured that if there was anything here of note, it would have been found by now.

Content that there's nothing else you can do here now – although you may come back later – you head over to meet the committee behind the Villages In Bloom competition. And they want to know if the event is still going to be going ahead. *Go to* **35** *and let's see how it goes.*

187

'Please leave me alone,' Heidi McLeish asks, her voice a cocktail of steel and distress. 'I'm done with it all. I've got to get away.'

'Ms McLeish,' you say authoritatively. 'Please. We need to talk.'

She slows as she reaches your car, and turns to you. 'It's the final straw. It really is this time. This whole place stinks.'

'I need you to tell me what's happened.'

'They've got exactly what they want, is what's happened. As usual.'

'What do you mean?'

'Well, that shortlist, for a start. What a huge surprise. There's Old Norton and Veronica Woollaston's mob on the shortlist. There's the Webber family on the shortlist. And as for Polly bloody Monk and Church Fields. She should be ashamed of herself.'

There's a lot to unpack here, and you're aware that the clock is ticking. There's a crowd back at the village hall, and you're going to need to get back to that quickly. What do you want to focus on?

What did she mean by 'as usual'? Go to **121.**
Why should Polly Monk be ashamed of herself? Go to **160.**
What's wrong with the Webbers and Veronica being on the shortlist? Go to **108.**

188

You walk around the plot of the grave and see if you can spot anything out of place. Try as you might, though, you see nothing of note. Apart from it being clean and kept well, it looks like nobody's disturbed it since the headstone was put in place.

Still, you take a closer look at the flower tributes. A simple card is enclosed with the largest of them, which reads 'All my love as always, V x'. A tidy, small arrangement, meanwhile, has no card included with it. And then the smallest of the three arrangements is tucked at the back, out of sight. Which is why you don't notice it at first.

Not the arrangement itself, but the card that's on it. You gasp as you read the handwritten words: 'Consider this card my insurance policy in case you come for me'.

Before you can wrap your head around what you've just read, a voice from behind you. 'Hello, Detective. How do you like my grave?'

You recoil in shock as the man behind you grabs you. You realize who it is, and quickly ascertain that you're in real trouble here.

And it doesn't get easier when you say his name out loud.
Head to **131**...

189

You're not quite sure how you've got yourself into this particular pickle, but you know there's no easy way out of it. You're faced with someone who could have killed you already, you realize, but for some reason hasn't. Moreover, he's offered you a way out. You take it.

You stand aside, and he takes the computer unit away. 'If you leave this house in the next two minutes, I'll be back for you,' he warns.

Not a chance, you think. You stand there for three, frozen to the spot as you realize just how close you came to it all being over. When you eventually pluck up the courage to go downstairs, he's long gone. You could tell that by the sound of a car urgently pulling away.

When you get to your own, you see that the tyres have been let down. An extra insurance policy, you reason. You call everything in, and a police car approaches barely ten minutes later. You figure you'd best head over to the competition announcement. Still, as you open the door to the passenger seat, you can't help but let out a huge gasp of breath.

You don't feel much closer to solving all of this. But at least you're still alive. You're taken to the village hall, where the competition continues at **63**.

190

As the car's alarm continues to blare out, you move at speed up the small path and try to find out where the clattering noise came from. The raging bleeping of the siren doesn't make it easy, but the task is made a bit more straightforward when you see a smashed wooden gate up ahead of you.

It's evidently the gate leading to the house opposite Veronica's, you note. You've disturbed someone in there, and they appear to be running at great speed up ahead of you. You figure you've little option but to give chase. They've got a comfortable head start on you, but you dig deep and are soon closing in on them. By their gait, you figure

they're a bit older than you, but they're in good shape.

The path winds back to the main road as you pursue the mystery figure past the extensive Villages In Bloom display. 'Catch him!' you scream at the officer watching from the bottom of Veronica's driveway, and he needs no second invitation. The two of you are soon in hot pursuit.

One of the initiatives in the Old Norton display for Villages In Bloom was a beautiful wooden windmill to greet the judges as they entered the village.

Much work had gone into the flower arrangement around it, and the sails of the windmill had been crafted out of steel by a local metalworker.

On the plus side, you get to experience first-hand the exceptional skill involved in their construction. The detail is quite something.

But it doesn't stop the sail hurting as it slices through the side of your head when you stumble and fall while giving chase. Even as the officer ahead of you apprehends the mystery figure, and will ultimately get to the bottom of some of the mysteries here, sadly you won't be around to see it. If you'd fallen just a few inches to the right, the beautiful ornamental sails may have just taken off your ear. But you didn't. And they didn't.

When the paperwork is completed, your cause of death will be listed as 'ornamental windmill'.

Detective: you failed to survive Midsomer. But at least you went out in style...

THE END

Go to p.293 to read your performance review.

191

You and DS Lambie head to his car. 'Where to now?' he asks as he steps inside. Your options are narrowing, that much is clear, and whatever lead there was here looks like it's now gone. 'I'm going to take a look at Veronica Woollaston's house: once last throw of the dice,' you suggest.

'You do that. I'll head back to the station to see if I can dig anything up from there,' he agrees.

Head to **163.**

192

You quickly turn around, trying to get any kind of advantage. You need to assess exactly what danger you're in, and what you can do to get out of it.

Thankfully, though, buying yourself time to assess the situation has avoided what could have been a rather unfortunate incident.

As you spin around, you come face to face with DS Brian Lambie, who you instantly recognize from Midsomer CID. He'd taken you around the station and introduced you to people when you went in for an induction session just last week, and you both relax as you work out who the other person is.

He regains his composure first.

'I didn't expect to see you here,' he says gruffly. DS Lambie feels a little less welcoming than when you first met, but you're conscious that you too are on edge. 'I didn't expect to be here, Sarge,' you reply. 'Don't suppose you've seen Veronica Woollaston, have you?'

'I was going to ask you the same question,' he sighs.

Both of you relax a little.

You explain what's happened on your first afternoon, and show him the slip of paper you found. You assume that he's following up the same case as you are – but you assume wrongly. There's more than one mystery here.

'I need to talk to her about the committee,' he opens up. 'I've been investigating it for a few months now.'

'What's the problem?'

'Well, our much-loved village committee appears to be on the verge of bankruptcy,' he says.

'Is that unusual? Aren't most village committees running things a bit hand to mouth?'

'Not this one,' he chuckles. 'Lack of funds hasn't been a problem since the Webber lot bailed them out ten years ago.'

'The Webber lot? Did they give the committee some money or something?'

'They certainly did that,' DS Lambie explains. 'They gave half a million pounds to it, to make sure it was never short.'

You take a breath. A village committee with those kind of funds?

'In fact, even last year, there was still at least six figures left.'

'You mean... they've spent over six figures in twelve months?' you remark, taken aback.

'Well, the money's gone somewhere. I had a hunch that the competition this weekend might be wrapped up in it all. And from what I've been hearing, it's not been cheap to put together.'

You explain how Mrs Woollaston left the coroner's in a hurry.

'Nothing wrong with that,' Lambie counters. 'A bit suspicious, but can't imagine her seeing a dead body again would be easy for her. After her husband.'

DS Lambie's radio bursts into life. You hear your name. 'I'll pass the message on,' he says.

'Well, that's solved a problem,' he says. 'Veronica Woollaston is at Norton village hall. And she's asking for you.'

You can head straight off to see her if you want to, or continue to explore the neighbourhood a little.

Off to the village hall, then! Drive over to **35**.
Take a moment to quiz the neighbours while you're here. You can do that over at **96**.

193

Time isn't on your side, you figure as you head towards the front door of the house. You leave Mr Thomas watching – and he's not altogether happy about it.

Still, you've got to try knocking the front door first. You can't just break in without at least seeing if someone is there. You walk up the short garden path. No door bell, no fancy ornamental knockers here. You tap at the door with your hand. You don't know whether to be relieved or disappointed that nobody seems to be inside.

You spot the wooden gate to the side of the house, and check your surroundings. There's no way around this: you're being filmed. Mr Thomas is holding his phone up, capturing what you're up to. 'Police,' you call over the fence to nobody in particular, in the hope that if, for whatever reason, there's an investigation into all of this, you've given yourself a bit of cover.

You take a breath and clamber over the gate into the badly kept garden and to the back door.

To your surprise, the back door's easy to open. It's not really locked: you can't tell if that's deliberate, or just disrepair. Either way, you open the door, hold up your identification card – just in case – and head inside.

The back door leads into a kitchen. Again, no sign of anyone about here. You note the small vase on the window sill and look inside. A spare key – to Monica's house, perhaps? But why?

You head upstairs. You need to be quick, and your anxiety levels increase when you hear a car pull up outside. You assume it's DS Lambie, and you can faintly hear the sound of a discussion breaking out.

Two rooms are in front of you. One appears to be a bedroom, the other a small study.

Which one do you want to check?
The bedroom? That's **151.**
The study? You need **165.**

194

As you exit the house, you make a beeline for DS Lambie, who's in deep conversation with the man you saw when you arrived.

'What's the problem?' you ask.

'This man, Mr Russ Thomas, has been filming you and taking photos of you.'

'Mr Thomas, is that true?'

'Yes,' he growls. 'You went in there without a warrant. I've watched enough television shows to know you're not allowed to do that.'

'I am in the middle of a murder enquiry, Mr Thomas.'

'Then you'll be able to talk your way out of it easily enough, then.'

'What did you do with the pictures?'

He suddenly goes quiet. DS Lambie pitches in: 'He's sent them to someone.'

'To who?' you ask Mr Thomas.

'To the person who told me to send him photos if anyone came snooping around the house.'

'Is this a recent arrangement?'

'Fairly.'

'Do you have a name of this person?'

'That's not how it works.'

'I need their number, Mr Thomas. Unless you want me to charge you with obstructing a murder enquiry.'

The thing about Russ Thomas is that while he'll happily take a few quid off a stranger to watch a house, he's less interested in getting himself into trouble. He reluctantly hands over the number, but not before he sends the images of you breaking into the house over to Midsomer CID. You sigh, and hope that doesn't get you into more trouble.

You call the station and hand over the number. Can they run a search on it? Well, they can. And a few minutes later when your call is returned, there's no information on the account holder. Just that the phone itself is active – and appears to be in the back garden of the house you've just left.

Head straight to the back of the house as fast as you can.
Go to **81**.
No, you need to be cautious. Sneak back and see what you can find. That'd be **118**.

⇝195⇜

You reverse back on yourself and head towards the picturesque countryside behind Veronica Woollaston's home. It's beautiful, you admit, as you breathe in the clean air. You have to step over the bodies of a couple of squirrels, who were presumably on the losing side of an argument with the local foxes.

Walking away from the house, it doesn't take long for you to lose sight of the building behind you as you explore the wooded area.

Did someone drop something here? Is there any sign of anything?

Then you spot it in the leaves ahead of you: a single training shoe. Around size ten or eleven, you'd guess just by looking at it. You don't have an evidence bag in your pocket so you don't want to disturb it.

You bend over to take a closer look at the shoe, noting the sound of wildlife just off to the side of you. But you're taken aback as something lands hard in your face. It throws you off kilter, and you shriek in horror when you see what it is.

One of the dead squirrels, its body stiff, has just been used as a projectile weapon, and smashed hard into your nose.

It hurts, but you're repulsed at the same time.

The second blow comes from behind. It can't be another squirrel, can it? You fervently hope not, but the effect of it makes those wishes immaterial. It knocks you forward, your head smashing into the tree trunk just ahead of you, a blow that knocks you out cold. Whoever your attacker is moves quickly, keen not to be noticed. They rain down a third blow on to you, just for good measure.

It's all over.

It'll be an hour or two before you're discovered, and it'll be touch and go whether you'll pull through.

As you're eventually whisked to hospital, where the doctors valiantly attempt to save you from the squirrel rigor mortis attack, a mysterious figure drives their little car off into the distance, never to be seen or heard of in Midsomer again...

THE END

Go to p.293 to read your performance review.

196

'That's a very serious thing to say, Mrs Webber,' you tell her as you slow the car down and park up just outside the village of Norton.

'I mean every word of it. This competition has been nothing but trouble since the day it was first announced.'

'I'm sorry I have to ask this,' you say, 'but do you have any idea who killed Peter Maddock?'

'No, I don't, Detective,' she says, slightly intolerantly. 'But I do know this: this whole place was a good deal friendlier before it all started. Just look at Veronica and Peter. They used to have tea together regularly. Then as soon as this all started and the petty rivalries started to kick in, everybody drifted apart.'

Interesting.

'This competition has brought the worst out in everybody, myself included I'm afraid. I've told my Geoff that he can't give them any more money after this. They just can't be trusted with it.'

'What about Veronica?'

'I'd trust her with my life, just not my bank balance,' Doreen Webber bites. 'She always seemed to go through money so quickly. I could never work out why. Mind you, she never liked the cheap things in life.'

'Do you think she's got something to do with Peter's death?'

'She's not a murderer, Detective. She's a very good friend. And while she may have a very ferocious bark, it's a lot more savage than her bite.'

'What do you think caused it then?'

'I think somebody wanted that prize money, and was willing to play unfair to get it. I can't prove it. I don't have any evidence. Just take that as a hunch from someone whose eyes and ears are a lot better than some around give credit for.'

You start the car and head towards Norton village hall again.

'I'd bet everything I own that without this competition opening up all these old wounds, Peter Maddock would still be with us. I really do believe that, Detective.'

You're beginning to think the same thing. But still: now there's the judges and their announcement to consider. You'd best get to the village hall at **63**.

197

Veronica Woollaston is sitting up in her bed when you arrive back at the hospital. She's still looking weak, and you're well aware that the pain medication the nurses have given her will leave her drifting in and out of consciousness for a while.

Still, she recognizes you and seems alert, even if she hardly looks delighted to see you.

'Just a few questions,' you say, almost apologetically. You're as keen to get this over with as Veronica.

Ask her why the committee is paying Williams Consulting by choosing **100**.
Or follow up why she's been paying Peter Maddock at **207**.

198

You walk down the road a little and, as you round a blind corner, you see the small vehicle tucked away, as if it's been hidden out of sight deliberately. From the outside it looks quite grubby, as if it hasn't been cleaned for months. Given the amount of dried mud on its sides, it's done its fair share of journeying around country roads too.

You can't tell by looking inside if the car has been abandoned in a hurry, but there's no sign of heat coming off the engine. Your best guess is that it's been here at least a couple of hours. Quite possibly a lot more.

Peering through the window, you see a collection of abandoned coffee cups and mint wrappers in the passenger footwell. You try the door, but it's locked. A pity. You wouldn't mind taking a look in the boot. The parcel shelf at the back of the car has been slightly dislodged, but you can't quite make out what's concealed beneath it.

You can't shake the feeling that it all feels a bit out of place. But what can you do? You could explore the small path the car has been hidden on. Do that at **114**.
Or – and you're very aware of the risks here – you could break into the car. For that, you need **141**.

199

This is it. This is the end stage. The final announcement of the winner. The end of the Midsomer Villages In Bloom competition.

The atmosphere is already testy, and the liberal amounts of homemade beverages that have been sold aren't bringing the temperature down.

It's Hazel O'Brien of the judging panel who steps to the stage this time. She's been given the clearly contentious job of announcing the winner to an already displeased crowd.

'Just hurry up and announce Old Norton,' heckles someone from the crowed, to general murmuring. They've got wind of a stitch-up, and Hazel O'Brien is the one who's about to take the flack one way or another.

She steps up to the microphone, clearly nervous. None of the committee nor the judging panel are anywhere near the stage, it seems. 'And the winner,' her quiet voice announces into the (thankfully quite powerful) microphone, 'is Old...'

Before she can even finish the sentence, she's drowned out by loud boos. This time, the crowd has turned. Not all of the words coming from the assembled mob are polite. She battles on regardless because, in truth, what else can she do? She's just got to get through this.

Monica Davies shuffles onto the stage and hands her another envelope.

Hazel tries to explain that she's now going to hand the prize money cheque over. Nobody from Old Norton seems particularly keen to come up and face the hostility of the crowd, but they need a picture for the newspaper. Reluctantly, when Old Norton's Elaine Deandy won't appear, it's Veronica Woollaston who quickly takes to the stage, takes the money, and leaves as quickly as she can.

But you notice something: there's a tear in her eye. Pushing through the decreasingly impressed crowd, you make your way towards her. 'It's all for nothing,' she sobs. 'They all hate me, and this cheque is worthless anyway.'

Ask her why it's worthless? Do so over at **178**.
Hmmm. You need to gather the judges together here. They're at **99**.

200

It's starting to get dark as you arrive back at Midsomer police station. It's been a very long first day, and you're no closer to uncovering the mystery behind Peter Maddock's untimely demise.

You head to your desk, which is completely empty, save for a computer that looks like it's seen better days. You've not been able to spend a minute here yet, and as you sit down you make a mental note to ask for a chair without a broken arm when all of this has settled down.

You input the login details you were given at your induction into the terminal in front of you. It reluctantly whirs into life and you find your way to the database you need. Naturally, the computer is in no rush to load anything, and you curse the spinning hourglass that seems etched into the screen. A message about 'trying to connect to the cloud' has you looking up hopefully.

Finally, you find what you're looking for. The information on Veronica Woollaston. It's quite sparse, you notice, save for an incident nearly two decades ago. The death of her husband, Frank. You grimace as a photograph slowly loads; it's not a pleasant one. Whatever went on between Frank Woollaston and a lawnmower on that fateful day, you're left in precious little doubt that it was a contest the latter firmly won. They presumably didn't make a visual identification of the body, that much you're sure of.

A closed casket funeral, understandably. He left a straightforward will too, with Veronica the sole beneficiary of his estate. They had no children. They'd even given the dog away when it soiled her begonias.

No wonder Veronica didn't want to hang around the morgue. But still: there's more to this. You feel it. You flick through the documents, looking for anything that could help, your eyes growing heavy as you do.

Tiredness overcomes you, and there's a big day ahead. You stare at the stained coffee pot on the side and reluctantly accept that sleep may be more useful than caffeine. You pack up and head back to your hotel, ready for a big day ahead. With nobody having called the competition off, it's going ahead...

Go and get some rest over on **67**. *The investigation will start again in the morning.*

201

You realize you're alone, and with no chance of getting any backup in the next few minutes, you decide to wait. From your vantage point behind the fence, you see the shadowy figure placing things under the compartment mat in the boot of the car. You can't make out what, but it must be quite small, whatever it is.

You steady your breathing and remain as quiet as you can. Instinctively, you reach for your phone and video what's happening as best you can. The light is low, but you never know.

They finish what they're doing and close the boot. Checking to see they're not being watched, they sneak back up the small road. Wherever they've been, it must be along there somewhere. Still, you leave it at least ten minutes – although it feels longer – before you allow yourself to move.

The car window has been left unlocked, so it takes little time to get access to the rear of the vehicle. Careful to video what you find, you open up the cover to the spare wheel compartment in the boot.

It doesn't take you long to find what must have been put here. In fact, it was very easy to find, as if this was evidence you were supposed to discover. Two small bottles with a clear liquid in. You'd wager poisonous liquid too, the kind of undetected toxin that might just have played a part in Monica Davies' demise.

It feels too simple. Maybe it is? Or maybe this is just where the murderer stored the bottles. They're not the kind of objects you want to be caught carrying on your person, after all. You look around as you ponder this, and realize how exposed you are on this quiet road. On the one hand, it makes the car itself easy to miss. On the other? Well, there are lots of disguised vantage points looking out on to it.

You shudder just a little as you consider this. Could this be planted here to see if anyone is on its owner's trail? There are more secluded places the car could be hidden. Or could it be some kind of a delaying tactic, you wonder? Something to distract the police while buying the perpetrator valuable time to slip away while everyone is focusing on something else? They must have known the car would be discovered and searched before it's towed away, and...

No. That can't be it. It doesn't add up. There must be something else. What if... what if the idea is to see if anyone is watching the car? To clear up a loose end? To try and draw someone out who's getting far too close to solving the crime?

What if they've put on a show, just in case you were watching them? Wha... Thump.

Your lifeless body hits the floor a matter of seconds, a broken fence post fatally interfacing with your head. Your body is dragged across the road and hidden behind the broken fence. The local wildlife lick their lips, ready to feast on you. They waste little time doing so.

Meanwhile, a shadowy murderer escapes Midsomer, never to be seen again...

THE END

Go to p.293 to read your performance review.

202

'Please wait here,' you ask Hazel, as you see DS Lambie at the door. He beckons you back to Monica Davies' house, to be met at her front door by the forensics officer. She's looking worried.

'What is it?'

'I'll need to run some lab work to back this up, but my initial feeling here is that Monica Davies didn't die of natural causes.'

A second murder? You press for further information.

'It was the way her teeth were slightly dislodged.'

'I noticed that. I just figured they'd fallen out a little.'

'More likely she was trying to spit them out.' She leads you back up the stairs and to the little bathroom off to the side of the landing. It shows signs of recent use. There are still fresh droplets of water in the sink from where it must have been used when Monica woke up. But also, there's a glass with a liquid in it, which presumably was where she'd left her dentures overnight.

'What are you suggesting?'

'I'm suggesting we get whatever's in that glass analysed, Detective.'

'I'm not following.'

'It's the only way to rule out what I'm fearing might have happened. I think Monica Davies may have been poisoned.'

You're taken a little aback. 'You're telling me that she died because of poisoned dentures?'

'I can't prove it. But that's looking a lot more likely than natural causes to me, Detective.'

You stop for a second to contemplate all of this, and then find DS Lambie. 'It's another murder enquiry,' you tell him, and bring him up to date. He sends the information back to the station. 'And whoever did it has used Hazel O'Brien's key to get in.'

A call comes in. It's Veronica Woollaston: she's conscious again and the doctors say you can ask her a few more questions. But you'll need to move fast: she's only awake for an hour or so at a time.

You need to get to Veronica! Go to **181**.
No, stay here and take a detailed look around Monica's house. That's **90**.

203

Polly Monk looks surprised at the question. 'I remember that Frank Woollaston was a nice man, doubly so if you could get in a conversation with him when his wife wasn't around. He was to me, anyway.'

'Were they an unhappy couple?'

'I couldn't tell you, just that they didn't appear to be a very happy one. At least not together. Everybody knew they rowed a lot.'

'How come?'

'Well, you couldn't really miss it. She had a ferocious temper back then. His in the end wasn't much better. I just think they always struggled to cover the bills more than they'd let on. They weren't the most forthcoming when money was required, let's just say that.'

'Nothing wrong with that, though?'

'True. It's just she's very different now. First to offer to pay the bill and all that, until recently at least. She clearly didn't do badly out of being a widow is all I'm saying. Well, not at first anyway.'

'Did anything ever strike you as suspicious?'

'A little too unsuspicious, I suppose. She grieved for a long time, rebuilt her life, built herself to where she is now. Did everything you'd expect someone to do, pretty much to the letter.'

'But isn't that just part of going through bereavement?'

'Of course. But she certainly changed a lot.'

You can't help thinking that Polly Monk is being a bit harsh here. But then maybe she's right. Maybe it is all a bit too perfect. Something to bear in mind as you head back to the village hall over at **199**.

204

'You talked about all the money dwindling away.'

'It did. Wouldn't be surprised if it's all gone after this weekend, too.'

'Where do you think it's gone?'

She laughs. 'Where does everything go? Under the eyes of Veronica Woollaston and her sacred committee. A committee that enables her to run the place however she wants. Everybody knows she's in charge, nobody wants to cross her.'

You try to steer her back on point. 'And the money?'

'That's the thing. It's all whispers, because nobody can get an exact figure off anybody. It was two or three years ago that they started cutting little bits of expenditure here and there. When the custard creams were taken away from committee meetings people thought things might be worse than anybody was letting on.'

'Who's the treasurer of the committee? Somebody must have oversight.'

She laughs again. 'Her best friend, of course. The deputy chair. Monica Davies.'

'Surely she has the figures?'

'Ask her yourself. But be warned. She's the worst head-nodder of the lot.'

You thank Polly Monk for her time and caution her not to leave the area in a hurry.

If you're going to pursue this line of enquiry, and try to get to the bottom of where the money's gone, you've got a small window. It's a couple of hours until the final announcement of the winner.
You can wait and head to the village hall for that at **199**.
Or you've got time to go to the station and do some digging around on Veronica and the finances at **5**.

205

You look to the house, as the man beside you continues to hold out his phone. He's watching you closely. He doesn't trust you, that much is clear.

Safety first this time, you concede. You can't break into the house without a warrant, and if you're looking for any other kind of justification you need to have someone here watching your back. Plus: who knows who's inside? Just because the place looks abandoned, it's far from certain that it is.

So you wait it out. You sit in your car as the time passes agonizingly slowly, deflecting the looks from residents and passers-by with as neutral and as serious an expression as you can. The man outside never stops watching you. At one point, he holds up his phone and seems to be taking photographs of you.

You wonder what he's doing with those. You continue waiting for Lambie. Five minutes turns into ten. Ten turns into fifteen. The man is still there. You decide you need to talk to him.

Exiting the car, the man suddenly puts his phone away. He does it so clumsily that your first thought is that he's no great loss to the spy trade. Still, you need to find out why he's watching you so closely.

His faded brown cardigan doesn't soften the fact that he's much bigger than you, and has the demeanour of someone who could look after themselves in a fight. Comforted by the knowledge that backup is on the way, you approach him again.

'Can I have your name, sir?'

'It's Thomas. Russ Thomas. Why?'

'Mr Thomas, why are you taking pictures of me?'

'Why are you sitting outside that house?'

'I'm waiting for my colleague to join me before I investigate it.'

No point lying, you figure.

'And I'm just making sure you're not up to something you shouldn't be.'

'What do you intend to do with the photographs?'

'Nothing now. Already done it.'

'Done what?'

'Sent them.'

'To who?'

'To the person who told me to take a photo of anyone hanging around the house.'

'Neighbourhood Watch?'

'You could say that.'

'And who is that person?'

'If he doesn't like the look of you, I'd imagine you'll find out soon enough.'

'Is that a threat?'

'No. Just common sense. I don't think he's the kind of person who takes kindly to people poking their beaks in.'

'What's in all of this for you?'

'Let's just say he looks after you.'

You fill in the gaps. Someone is slipping Russ Thomas a few quid to watch the property. But who?

You need to push this and get a name. That's **4**.
A different approach: try appealing to his better nature – it is a murder enquiry, after all. Go to **166**.

206

Reluctantly, you realize that Veronica is probably the person you need to talk to. She's the one where your trail started this afternoon, and she's the one who, for reasons you've not worked out yet, is wrapped up in what's been going on so far.

She's also the person everyone hopes will be able to change your mind. 'Shall we go and have a word in private, Detective?', she asks, with enough grit in her voice to suggest it wouldn't be a good idea to say no.

You follow her through one of the side doors of the village hall and down a small corridor. At the end is a further door that leads to a tiny office. 'We'll get some privacy here,' she states calmly as she gestures you in.

'What is it, Mrs Woollaston?' you say, slightly irritated by the whole charade. Surprisingly, that's when she does something you're really not expecting. Veronica starts to cry. Not a full-on cry. But a few sobs and a couple of tears for good measure. Is she manipulating you, or is this genuine?

She composes herself. 'I'd like you to reconsider,' she asks, just an undercurrent of humanity now present in her tone. 'This competition really means the world to me.'

'A man is dead, Mrs Woollaston,' you remind her.

'I know, Detective,' she says, a fresh tear forming. 'And I've been threatened too.'

Threatened? You ask her to explain.

'The committee is in trouble,' she tells you. 'We're nearly out of money. We need this competition to happen.'

'I can understand that,' you concede, but not giving ground. 'But how does that equate to you getting threatened?'

'I had a phone call,' she tells you. Her veneer is slipping a little. You leave a pause, inviting her to continue her story.

'Shortly before you arrived this morning. Somebody called my house.'

'What did they say?'

'Make sure it happens,' she sobs. 'And then you told me what happened to poor Peter.'

She pauses.

'I'm scared, Detective.'

Now what?

Do you let this competition go ahead? It sounds like there's big trouble if it doesn't. Just give them what they want, and head back to your hotel for the night. Best go to **67**.

This is getting too big for just one person now. Veronica surely needs to go to the police station. Go to **21**.

No. This competition is over. There's too much danger now, and once they know at the station what's been going on, there no way they'll disagree. Head to your car. Go to **214**.

207

'I need to talk to you about a bank statement or two,' you say, to Veronica's obvious concern. She tries to give you a neutral look, but you see the flash of worry in her eyes.

'What statement?' she says, wincing at the pain she's still obviously in.

'I've come into possession of some of Peter Maddock's bank statements, Mrs Woollaston. And there appears to be a regular flow of payments from you to him.'

She's still trying to hold it together, but she knows she's in trouble here.

'Oh.'

'I'm puzzled, Mrs Woollaston. When we first met, you tried to tell me you barely knew Peter Maddock. Now I've discovered that you didn't just know him, you were paying him what looks like a monthly sum of money. Do you understand how serious this is, Mrs Woollaston? I've got documentation here that tells me you were paying a man who has just been murdered.'

Tears start forming in her eyes this time. There's panic in her voice, and the beeping from the machine next to her gains momentum.

'I–I...'

'I think it's time you told me everything, Mrs Woollaston.'

Finally, she opens up.

'He was blackmailing me.'

'Why?'

'Because he knew. He knew everything.'

'What did he know?'

'About Frank. He knew about Frank.'

As she begins to tell you the story, you struggle to wrap your head around the network of secrets and lies here. But it turns out that Veronica's much-loved, long-lost husband is neither much-loved nor long-lost. In fact, he's very much alive.

She tells you about how being married to Frank Woollaston was far from the perfect life it appeared. Granted, he loved her and was very protective. But he also had a habit of straying, and of losing their money on business ventures that misfired. And eventually, with their marriage on the verge of collapse, he came up with one last can't-fail scheme. With a swift backhander to a retiring coroner, he faked his death, with the help of Peter Maddock.

'How did he know Peter?'

'They knew each other from the local theatre group.'

'And Peter has been blackmailing you?'

She nods. She explains how as Peter's own financial situation got more and more stretched, he started asking for more and more money – to the point where Veronica's now struggling to make ends meet any more.

'And Frank?'

'I'm scared,' she admits. 'I'm really scared.'

'Do you think Frank killed Peter Maddock? And Monica Davies?'

The tears come flooding out now, and Veronica nods her head. 'And I think he's coming back for me.'

'Did he do this to you?'

She nods.

'And he's still in the area?'

She nods again.

But still: she's complicit here, isn't she? Isn't all this a convenient way to get her out of a spot?

This one's up to you, Detective.
Get the message to HQ that Frank is alive at **11**.
It's time to arrest Veronica. She's led you a merry dance and it has to stop. Go to **74**.

208

You switch your phone's ringer off and put it back into your pocket.

'You sure you should be doing that?'

'Not really. But do you think I have a lot of choice?'

DS Lambie doesn't look too convinced, but you quickly turn your attention to the pile of bank statements. You flick through them quickly, and it doesn't take long to spot some pretty sizeable leads.

Two things stand out. Firstly, Peter Maddock's own bank statement is at the back of the collection of papers, and he seems to have been getting regular payments – which have been growing in size – from a Mrs V I Woollaston.

And then there's the committee's financial records. They make for grim reading, even at a superficial glance. A six-figure balance has been heavily depleted in the last two years, and the balance is teetering just a few pounds above zero. Where on earth can all the money have gone? You've suspected for a while that the Villages In Bloom might be a white elephant, and that seems to be where the bulk of the funds are directed. Well, you assume so: a company called Williams Consulting is the recipient of the lion's share of it.

But who is that company? And why was Veronica sending Peter money? Right at the start of this investigation, she pretended she barely knew him. Now she appears to be bankrolling him.

The Chief Inspector won't wait forever for you to get in touch. You need to pick which of these leads to follow.

Do a search for Williams Consulting by calling at **30**.
Head on over to the hospital and talk to Veronica Woollaston again at **100**.

209

It soon becomes very clear that Trevor Webber wasn't kidding. As you drive to the village of Norton Green to talk to his parents, a huge house comes into view. In an area where property prices are hardly frugal, you'll do well to find a dwelling that compares to this one.

It takes a little time to get to the front door, not just because the entrance to the long driveway is down a winding track. You've also got to wait for someone to let you in. You press the buzzer and hold up your ID to the small camera, then the huge metal gates creak open and allow your car onto the property.

You park up and head to the sizeable front doors. You're met there by Geoff Webber, a man who gives the appearance of someone in their seventies. He certainly dresses that way. Is that a string vest underneath his shirt?

He introduces himself and invites you in, keen to help. 'My wife, Alice, has gone to bed, I'm afraid. And I gather you've met Trevor.'

'He called?'

'He did,' Geoff laughs. 'I'm guessing you saw the hot-headed version of him.'

'A little.'

'He can get like that. He's a good kid really. He just thinks we're spending his inheritance.'

'And are you?'

'Absolutely,' Geoff Webber roars.

He's good company, alert and helpful. He gives you some useful background, too. Of how he and his wife have always loved village life, and when they made their fortune through their chain of pubs, their brewery and their other businesses, they were always determined to give something back. 'Once we'd got the house, what else did we really need?'

They'd bankrolled the village committee to secure its future, paid for the village hall in Norton and helped out with the Villages In Bloom competition.

'I'm sorry to ask,' you say, realizing that half an hour has passed and you've not got any closer to what you came for. 'I just need to follow up about a typewriter.'

'Is Trevor still moaning about that? I did try and fix it for him.'

'He said it was broken.'

'He's absolutely right about that. It's probably still in the shed, if you want to see what a knackered old typewriter looks like.'

Do you need to see it? He might get a little miffed that you don't believe him – but what if they're lying about it being broken? *That option is at* **167**.

While he's feeling chatty, ask him about his investment in the village committee. That's at **43**.

210

Conscious that you need to be reporting back to the station quickly – the Chief Inspector won't wait forever – your gut instinct tells you that you might actually have a chance to resolve the case here. Right now. The details of the blackmail aren't that important for the moment, you reason. No: there's a murderer out there, and it might just be that Veronica knows who's responsible.

'I have to ask you, Mrs Woollaston: do you know who killed Peter Maddock?'

She looks at you, shock registering in her eyes.

'What?'

'Do you know who killed Peter Maddock?'

'Detective, I am not proud of everything I've done. I've got to live with that. But don't think for a minute think I've got any knowledge of that man's death.'

She starts to clam up, angry at the turn the conversation has taken.

'Mrs Woolla...'

'I didn't like Peter Maddock, Detective. He has made my life hell for the last few years,' she splutters. 'But that's a long way away from...'

You'd almost forgotten that she was still hooked up to monitoring technology, and the intensifying of beeps from the machine next to her alerts the nursing staff. A nurse enters the room, takes one look at Veronica getting flustered and clearly unhappy, and looks back at you. 'You'll have to leave.'

You already know that, and your phone continues to demand your attention. You can't put this off any longer – it's time to go and see the clearly impatient Chief Inspector. Off you go to **80.**

211

You figure that all you've got left in your corner here is the truth, and you may as well tell it. 'Sir, I'm not suggesting that I've gone about things in the most orthodox manner...'

'That's some understatement, Detective.'

'But please: let me follow this through. I think I've got a lead on the financial problems of either Monica Davies, or the committee itself. Heck, it might even be both.'

'Do I want to know how you've procured this lead?'

'Probably not,' you admit. 'But at least give me a few hours to see it through. I'll stay within the lines, but we might not have much time to get to the bottom of all of this.'

'A couple of hours,' he says. 'But we're going to have to have a conversation about this video I've been sent, and it won't be an easy one.'

'I understand,' you say, and you end the call.

'He giving you a hard time?'

'Yeah, you could say that. We've not got long. Here's what I got out of the house in Bunbury.'

You quickly start to flick through the collection of bank statements. They make for stark reading. A committee that was once in credit to the tune of six figures has seen its bank balance deplete to practically nothing. A whole series of payments relating to the Villages In Bloom competition, the majority of which are going to a company called Williams Consulting. But what on earth could that be?

A statement at the back of the pile, meanwhile, belongs to Peter Maddock. And it turns out he's been receiving sizeable payments from a Mrs V I Woollaston.

Time is ticking. Do you run a search for Williams Consulting? Try **30.**
Or do you try to find out more from Veronica? You need **197.**

212

You remember your first visit to this house, where this all started. Back then, you seemed to have to wait an age for Veronica Woollaston to unbolt the numerous locks and chains before she could open her front door. This time, you spot one of your colleagues outside her house in the police car, and they tell you the door's already open.

There's a small flurry of activity behind it. Scene-of-crime officers are doing their best to gather what they can, but you soon glean that there's really not a lot to work with here. Apparently Veronica says she was attacked as she came downstairs to get a glass of water in the middle of the night. Curiously, though, there's no obvious sign of a struggle here. There's a broken glass on the floor, certainly, but nothing else seems out of place.

Chatting to the officers examining the scene, you also learn that there wasn't any sign of forced entry. Whoever it was, the most likely way they got in was through the back door, which Veronica must have forgotten to lock. It doesn't sound like her, but in the absence of anything more concrete it seems the most logical working theory.

Or does it?

At least it's backed up by some fresh footprints running through her garden and to a fence leading to open fields the other side. Casts are being taken, but the best you've learned so far is they're likely a male size ten or eleven.

You poke around the house a little, but you have an overriding feeling that what's not here is more interesting than what is. Do you want to double-check this and find the officer who was first on the scene? Go to **136.**
Or head back outside and check out that small car you saw parked up? Pop over to **198.**

213

You head towards the back of the church and crouch between a row of pews. You sit there waiting. And waiting. And waiting. You hear the noise of someone banging about, but then they seem to head outside. Are they looking for something? Are they not interested in you? That seems to be the case, you conclude, as you wait another 15 minutes to see if they return. No sign.

You get up and head to the small door again. You press your ear to it and hear nothing. It takes some force, but you break it down and follow the small corridor to an already-open fire exit.

Cautiously, you creep outside, but… nothing. Whoever it was seems to have gone. But what did they want?

You gaze over at Frank Woollaston's grave, just to check. The only thing you notice is that the flower arrangements that were on it are now missing. Will you ever find out why?

Satisfied that there's nothing else to see here, you reluctantly decide your only lead left is the finale of the competition itself. And that's where you must head. It's time for **199**.

214

Leaving an unhappy committee behind you, you leave the village hall. 'We can't keep going round in circles on this,' you say. 'Like it or not, there's a murderer out there somewhere. And I'd rather make myself unpopular and keep everyone safe than carry on regardless with your competition. I'm very sorry, I have to insist that the competition cannot go on.'

There are murmurs about taking it up with your superiors, of course, but nothing else is going to be decided here. Exhausted, you head back to your car. With the competition not happening, at the very least it means tomorrow you can concentrate on trying to solve the murder.

As you get into the driver's seat, you allow yourself to exhale a little. You know you've done the right thing by holding your ground, but this isn't how you wanted your first day to turn out. Still, what choice did you have? These people are hardly being co-operative.

You put the key in the ignition and you're about to turn it when you spot it. A small piece of paper, tucked inside your windscreen wiper. Virtually unseeable from the outside, and you barely saw it from within. You quickly look around. Nobody's about. You step out of the car, retrieve the piece of paper, and slip back inside the vehicle. You shut the door and check you're alone.

And then you unfold it. A typed note, and a very simple one. The message is straightforward: 'Meet me around the back of your hotel at 11pm. If you tell a soul, I won't be there. Come alone.'

There goes any chance you had of an early night.
What do you do?
There's no way you're chancing it by going on your own.
Report in and ask for backup. Go to **102.**
Head to the meeting alone, as requested. Nothing could go wrong, right? Let's see how that goes over at **70.**

215

'Can I just have a quick look?' you ask as you get to your feet.

'Help yourself. I'll have hidden them at the end of the row,' she grins.

It doesn't take long to find them. Three or four discs marked Norton Players. And she's right: they look really professional. The productions here are *Macbeth*, *Dracula*, *The Mousetrap* and *Mother Goose*. You suspect the latter was the local pantomime.

'They went to town on these, didn't they?'

'They did. To be fair to them, they sold well as well. Frank was always really proud of them, right down to the little book tucked inside.'

You open the case, and a small pamphlet is indeed included. A mini-programme, listing the full cast and crew. You note the name of Peter Maddock on Special Effects duty. You peruse the stills from the production on the box as well.

'This one looks a bit bloody,' you remark.

'It all had to be right. He never went over the top, but he always wanted it to be believable.'

'This Dracula definitely looks believable.'

'Caused a ruckus, that one. Frightened some of the younger members of the audience, shall we say. Borrow the disc and take a look. You'll see what I mean.'

You thank her, but figure you don't need to borrow it. You could still ask Shirley about Veronica, though, at **49**. *Or it might be time to head to the big finale back at Norton? That's over at* **199**.

216

As you process everything Veronica has just told you, you go for the unasked question.

'Did you have any involvement in the death of your husband, Mrs Woollaston?'

Had this been normal circumstances, Veronica would have batted the question off without thinking twice. But as soon as she stops and has to think about her answer, you both know that she's giving something away.

She knows the game is up.

'Yes,' she nods.

'I'm afraid I have to ask this, Mrs Woollaston. Did you murder your husband?'

'No,' she replies quietly.

'No?'

'No. I'm not perfect, Detective, but I'm not a murderer.'

'Do you know who did?'

Another tear streams down her cheek.

'Nobody did.'

'I'm not following, Mrs Woollaston. There were suspicions over his death, we've agreed on that. But now you're saying nobody killed him?'

'No, Detective, you don't get it.'

'Help me out.'

She looks you square in the eye, bruises around the side of her face. 'He's not dead, Detective.'

Not dead? You need to get this information to the station urgently. Call **11.**

Veronica is leading you a merry dance here. Arrest her and get this case over with. Go to **74.**

217

On your travels around Midsomer, you've had so many people talking about things that you've got no concrete evidence for. You can't risk not capturing what's going on here, and try to shift the phone quietly to a more open place. You just hope that someone is listening on the other end of the call.

But you've got another problem here. Your movements are becoming more stilted, presumably as a result of the toxin in your system. Your attempt to shuffle your phone to a more advantageous position results in you knocking it to the floor. Even if you wanted to retrieve it quickly, you couldn't. Your body just isn't playing ball.

Frank Woollaston is on it in a flash, quickly realizing what you've done. He ends the call and looks at you.

'I presume that somebody on the other end of that phone knows I'm here now,' he remarks matter-of-factly.

He turns to Veronica. 'I'm sorry, V. This isn't the goodbye I wanted. Please know I loved you, I still love you, and I never wanted you to get hurt. I only wanted the best for you.'

Then it's back to you. He removes the SIM card from your phone and pockets it. 'I think I'll just leave you here, Detective. Hopefully someone will find you in time, but you'll understand that I can't take that chance.' He takes one last glance at the pair of you and slips out of the room.

The person who saved you was Veronica.

It's several hours before you regain consciousness, but you learn that Veronica pressed the button by the side of her bed to call for attention once Frank had left. They weren't quick enough to stop him, but they did get there in time to save you.

It's one consolation as your investigation runs out of road: that there were only two murders in Midsomer this weekend, instead of three.

By the time the CCTV camera footage is checked, people are questioned and a search is scrambled, Frank Woollaston is a long way away. His cluttered little car moves swiftly through the winding roads, making full use of its head start.

As you sit up in a hospital bed yourself, Frank Woollaston has left Midsomer for the last time, and the murders, even though you don't know it at the time, are destined to remain unsolved.

Better luck next time...

THE END

Go to p.293 to read your performance review.

218

You try looking for Polly Monk, but you soon conclude she must be inside the village hall.

Still, a stroke of luck: it looks like the village representatives are coming out at last. The official announcement from the judges must be imminent, and you swoop in to try and grab two minutes of Polly's time.

'What can I help you with, Detective?'

'I just wondered what you and Trevor Webber were, well, "disagreeing" about?'

'Oh. You saw that.'

'I didn't. Plenty of other people did.'

'And plenty of other people have been on the end of Mr Webber's tongue this week too, I'd imagine. There's a young man who likes to stir things up, no matter how over the line he goes.'

'How over the line did he go?'

'I think, Detective, when you start throwing around unfounded accusations of people sabotaging other village's displays, that goes over the mark.'

She pauses, and catches herself, allowing herself to calm down a little. You note her face is going a raging crimson colour.

'I won't deny that we all want to win this thing. Heck, if you look at what the prize is – the sheer amount of money at stake – who *wouldn't* want to win this thing? But I think most of us – and I do not include Trevor Webber in this – see that the villages and the good that this is supposed to do for them is far more important than anyone's individual gain.'

'Do you know anything about the sabotage?' you quickly ask, not wanting that to get lost in the conversation.

'Absolutely nothing,' she snaps. 'Will that be all?'

It will be for the minute: the doors to the village hall are opening again. It finally looks like the announcement – or at least some kind of announcement – is about to be made.

Off to **145**...

219

'He knew about Frank?' you ask, genuinely puzzled. 'Knew what about him?'

She pauses. Takes a breath. Then hits you with the revelation. 'Knew that Frank was alive.'

It hangs in the air, and your brain fights to process it.

'I think you'd better tell me the full story, Mrs Woollaston.'

Finally, she does, and it's an incredible tale. As unpleasant as Frank was to her, it turns out he was fiercely protective of Veronica. With their marriage in trouble, wracked with guilt over his many affairs and with their money running short, he concocted a scheme and roped in Peter to help. No, Frank didn't die on that fateful day nearly two decades ago. The last of their savings was spent to pay off a retiring coroner, and Veronica was able to turn her life around with the policy payout she eventually received.

Frank pretty much left her alone, but then Peter began to need money. He started blackmailing her, infrequently at first, but then more and more regularly. Eventually, she couldn't keep up with the payments, and started to run out of money herself.

Frank would get in touch every now and then, she explained, and eventually learned what Peter was up to.

'Do you think Frank killed him?'

'I don't know, Detective. I honestly don't know. I'm so scared.'

As she should be.

It's a challenge to work out exactly what Veronica Woollaston will be charged with. For now, though, Frank Woollaston is alive – and out there somewhere.

You believe this? You need to get the message out!
Tell the station that Frank is alive at **11**.
Not buying it. Veronica's guilty as hell – arrest her. That's **74**.

YOUR PERFORMANCE REVIEW

There are many different possible endings to your Midsomer adventure. Playing through the book again and making different decisions might lead you to uncover more secrets.

If you want a sense of how much of it you discovered, and suggestions for improvement, then step this way for your performance review.

Look for the numbered section you ended on to find out what the Chief Inspector wrote in your personnel file.

14: LOST IN SERVICE

The detective certainly showed promise and appeared to track down the murder. They had potential, but their death makes them an unviable candidate for promotion.

Recommended course of action: Readvertise their job.

15: FAULTLESS

The detective did superb work, not only solving the case, but also making a successful arrest. They also went over and above the call of duty and uncovered a buried mystery from 20 years ago. A real find, and surely destined for greater things.

Recommended course of action: Promotion, and a commendation too.

19: MAIN CASE SOLVED, OTHER LINES OF ENQUIRY STILL OPEN

The detective recovered quickly from their poisoning and uncovered the secret of one Mr F Woollaston. A successful arrest. A few loose threads, but a good performance, all things considered. Can't help feeling Veronica and the committee got off light, though...

Recommended course of action: Promotion.

20: BOTH DISAPPOINTING AND DEAD

A very disappointing recruit. Notwithstanding the fact that the detective is now dead, they didn't even last their first day, and solved nothing. Next of kin informed.

Recommended course of action: Let's just get on with the job interviews for their replacement.

26: MAIN CASE SOLVED, OTHER LINES OF ENQUIRY STILL OPEN

Conviction secured against Mr Woollaston. No charges filed against any other suspect. Murder case itself solved. Nagging feeling that there was more waiting to be uncovered – Veronica Wollaston seems to have got off easy.

Recommended course of action: Note of commendation put on file.

44: ALIVE, BUT SHOULD CONSIDER ANOTHER LINE OF WORK

The detective showed promise, but that petered out quickly enough. Hasty, and significant concerns were raised over their judgement and actions. Not sure I'd trust them with a cup of coffee after this case.

Recommended course of action: Can we transfer them back to where they came from?

54: MINOR SUCCESS, BUT MURDER CASE STILL OPEN

Some promise here. It was always going to be a difficult case to solve, and it remains open. Two significant arrests on other matters. Pretty decent result for a first case, and the detective deserves encouragement.

Recommended course of action: Commendation from the Chief Inspector. Might need a senior partner for next few cases, though.

55: CASE UNSOLVED, DETECTIVE INJURED, EXPECTED TO MAKE RECOVERY

Had high hopes for this one. The detective was good at following instincts, but less accomplished at getting out of the way of heavy objects. Case unsolved. Jury still out on the detective.

Recommended course of action: Keep the detective on desk duty until they're settled.

68: DIED HEROICALLY. CASE UNSOLVED.

A tragedy. The detective was good at following their instincts and showed real promise. Sadly, their cavalier approach to dangerous situations was their undoing. The case remains unsolved.

Recommended course of action: Send flowers, advertise the position again.

74: NOT CUT OUT TO BE A POLICE DETECTIVE

A frustrating performance from our new detective. They managed to get close to solving the case, but couldn't come up with either the necessary evidence or an arrest. Flattered to deceive.

Recommended course of action: Send them back to uniform.

76: LOST IN THE LINE OF DUTY. AVOIDABLE DEATH.

Made some progress, and then shot themselves in the foot by not taking basic safety precautions. A cautionary lesson for future detectives.

Recommended course of action: Advertise for a new detective. Get HR to do a health and safety check on computer equipment.

80: STILL ALIVE. NOT MUCH OF AN ASSET TO THE DEPARTMENT.

All a bit piecemeal. Lacked haste and judgement. Made some progress, but it'll be a long time before we're promoting this one.

Recommended course of action: Send on training courses. Lots of training courses.

81: HUGELY DISAPPOINTING

Awful. Any progress completely undermined by reckless endangerment. Resignation accepted. Taxi booked to take them to station.

Recommended course of action: Burn this file and let us not speak of them again.

91: LOST IN THE LINE OF DUTY. CASE STILL OPEN.

Put themselves in danger without calling for any support. Didn't share information. Failed to avoid wheelbarrow. Personal effects sent to relatives. Case unsolved.

Recommended course of action: Send HR memo about quality of recruiting processes.

94: MAIN CASE SOLVED, SOME LINES OF ENQUIRY STILL OPEN

Real promise here. Successful arrest and conviction secured. Needs support in covering off details and ensuring all loose ends tied up. Did Veronica know more, for instance?

Recommended course of action: Assign another murder case, should one come up.

97: MAIN CASE SOLVED, SOME LINES OF ENQUIRY STILL OPEN

Good performance on first case – a good result. Arrest secured, case solved. Details still missing, and question marks over not being able to get the accused to reveal more details. Questions over Veronica and that committee, too. Still, promising.

Recommended course of action: Fast-track for promotion. With guidance, this one could go far.

101: FAULTLESS. THEY'LL BE RUNNING THE DEPARTMENT ONE DAY.

Hard to think what more they could have done. Two murders solved, conviction secured, another arrest imminent on other matters. One of the best detectives we've ever had.

Recommended course of action: Promotion, commendation and Barnaby's old desk.

104: A SAD LOSS. CASE UNSOLVED.

Whatever promise the detective showed was undermined by a lack of forward planning. Demonstrated intuitive detective skills, but missed obvious dangers. They will be missed.

Recommended course of action: Let's tell the next of kin that they were shot or something. They don't need to know the details.

128: ONE OF THE WORST CASE PERFORMANCES WE'VE EVER HAD

Case unsolved. Assaulted one of our officers. Chief Inspector stopped it getting in the papers. DS Lambie taking enforced early retirement on health grounds. A disaster.

Recommended course of action: Accept the detective's resignation. Quickly.

133: BRAVE, BUT ULTIMATELY UNSUITED TO THIS LINE OF WORK. ALSO: DEAD

Any progress was undermined by lack of physical agility. Tragically, it cost the detective their life. Case remains open and unsolved.

Recommended course of action: Take potatoes off the menu at the canteen for a while, as a sign of respect.

140: CASE UNSOLVED. DETECTIVE LOST.

A sad loss to the department. Clearly had some nous, but lacked basic common sense. Case remains unsolved and needs reassigning.

Recommended course of action: We might need to cover up the cause of death here. Switch the office computers to laptops.

142: CASE REMAINS UNSOLVED, AND LITTLE CHANCE OF THAT CHANGING

A real disappointment. After some initial promise, the detective's first case remains open, with no obvious leads and no realistic chance of it being solved.

Recommended course of action: Assign traffic duty. Get them away from future murder investigations.

147: INJURED IN THE LINE OF DUTY, MURDERER ESCAPED

The detective got close to solving the case, but their naivety led to the murderer being able to escape. Enquiries are ongoing; we don't have much hope of a result.

Recommended course of action: Sign them off. Just in case whatever they were drugged with is still in their system.

162: INJURED, CASE UNSOLVED, MURDERER ON THE LOOSE

Case remains open, and countywide alert issued for Mr Woollaston. Detective is expected to make a full recovery in time.

Recommended course of action: Signed off for the foreseeable future. See if there's a more capable detective we can put on the case.

175: CASE APPEARS CLOSED. OTHER LINES OF ENQUIRY NEED FOLLOWING UP

While we couldn't level charges, it seems clear who the murderer was. We consider the case closed, even though the suspect is now deceased. Lack of clear evidence means formal conviction impossible.

Recommended course of action: Further training required, but a good candidate for future promotion.

180: CASE STILL OPEN, NO ARRESTS MADE

A bit hit and miss. Made some progress, couldn't close the case. Chances of successfully solving it now look slim. Not the best new detective we've had.

Recommended course of action: Keep them in post, don't say no if they ask for a transfer.

190: DETECTIVE LOST, CLOSED COFFIN RECOMMENDED

We mourn the loss of the detective, who looked to be making some progress, but failed to spot what was ultimately under their nose. An ornamental windmill, in this case.

Recommended course of action: Beef up health and safety requirements around future floral exhibits.

195: FOOLHARDY. MURDERER ESCAPED. CASE STILL OPEN.

A rank amateur. Walked into danger with no call for backup or adequate self-protection. Tragic waste of life. Was never cut out to be a detective.

Recommended course of action: Better recruitment. Might want to look into the state of the squirrel population.

201: THEY SHALL BE MISSED. CASE STILL OPEN.

Hard to know where to start. Made significant progress on the case, and then left themselves open to attack. And were attacked.

Recommended course of action: Condolences to family, make sure the story doesn't make the newspapers.

217: ALIVE, BUT NO REAL SIGN OF CASE BEING SOLVED.

Got agonizingly close to an arrest. Alert sent out around county for Mr Woollaston. Hopes of arrest not high. Murders unsolved.

Recommended course of action: Full health check, keep the detective on light duties.

Notes

CASE CLOSED